Slow Down
and
Lighten Up

Letting Go of Stress and Tension

Bob Van Oosterhout, M.A., LMSW, LLP

Slow Down and Lighten Up:
Letting Go of Stress and Tension 2nd Edition
by Bob Van Oosterhout

Library of Congress Control Number: 2016905602
ISBN 2nd edition   978-0-9707781-1-6
1. Stress Management. 2. Balance 3. Anxiety
4. Healthy Living 5. Counseling/Psychology

1st Edition copyright 2001
ISBN-10: 0-9707781-0-4   ISBN-13: 978-0970778109

Printed in the United States of America

Illustrations by Katherine Darnell
www.kldarnell.com/

Cover design by Vanya Prokopovich

Cover photograph by Arnold Paul, Creative Common
http://creativecommons.org/licenses/by-sa/4.0/
No changes were made to the photograph

Published by Good Enough Publishing, Harrison, MI 48625
website www.bobvanoosterhout.com
email: goodenoughpublishing@gmail.com

Dedicated to the memory of:
Sano Ferrara
a man who saw value and opportunity
in each moment
and
Rosalyn Nowak
a woman who saw God's hand everywhere

Changes to 2nd Edition
April 2016

The cover was changed. Terms were updated, phrasing clarified, and a summary was added to the end of the book. The terms "Natural Rhythmic Breathing" and "Thought Refocusing" replaced "Diaphragmatic Breathing" and "Thought Focusing" used in the first edition.

Acknowledgments

I am indebted to the many clients, students, and workshop participants who have shared their struggles in ways that made it possible for us to learn from each other.

Contents

Introduction

Stress Can Be Like a Whirlwind

Stress can turn our lives into whirlwinds. Demands press in on us from all sides. We seem to spin 'round and 'round until we gradually lose balance and focus.

Whirlwinds easily become a way of life. We get so caught up in our stressors that it feels as though we're running behind and in circles at the same time. Self-perpetuating whirlwinds rev us up and wear us down. They sap our energy and disrupt our peace of mind. They toss us around until it feels as though we're riding on a fast-moving bus that stops only to refuel and never has time for regular maintenance. Eventually stress whirlwinds throw us into a collapsed heap without energy or motivation to keep going.

Stress that is not managed continues to build. This leads to inefficiency, ineffectiveness, loss, and, sometimes, danger to self or others. The consequences of long term stress include anxiety, depression, and poor health, in addition to losing our peace of mind and satisfaction with life. The whirlwind of stress affects our health, work, pleasure, and relationships. It keeps us from realizing our full potential and the meaning and purpose of our lives.

Understanding, Managing, and Preventing

This book is a whirlwind-prevention-and-recovery manual. Its purpose is to help us understand how stress whirlwinds develop while providing a set of basic tools and principles to keep stress from dominating our lives. The goal is to learn how to slow down enough so we can get our bearings and make choices that lead to improved health, life satisfaction, and peace of mind.

Stress whirlwinds twist and tie us in knots. The first step is to stop pulling on the knot, and then to see how the various threads are tangled together. The next step is to gradually loosen and untangle the strings while taking care not to snarl them again. The deeper recesses of the knot become evident after the surface snarls are free. We repeat this many times until gradually we learn how to keep things loose and eventually how to prevent the knot from forming again. Then we move to the next knot.

I have found that most things are easier to deal with once we understand how they work. One of the first things I do when counseling people who are struggling with stress, anxiety, depression, or PTSD is explain, in simple terms, what is happening to their body, mind, and emotions. Seeing the larger picture can help take us out of our current whirlwind for a moment. I also find it helpful to focus first on the most immediate and pressing problems. Learning to manage the immediate situation more effectively gives us the skills and confidence to take on more difficult and deeply entrenched areas of tension. As we understand more and manage more effectively, we can recognize patterns, anticipate problems, and prevent them from creating stress in our lives.

Stress, Anxiety and Depression

The basic explanations, skills, and principles that I have found to be effective in dealing with stress also play an important role in recovery from anxiety, depression, and PTSD. A build up of physical, mental, and emotional tension is a common factor in all three disorders. In counseling people who have survived severe trauma, I have learned that staying "at the surface" is the most effective way to get at deeper problems. Once immediate problems are worked through, any deep-seated issues that are present seem to gradually come up. The same tools and approaches seem to be effective in dealing with both immediate and long-term, deep-seated problems.

A Process of Improvement

I believe that the key to effectively understanding, managing, and preventing stress is to see our efforts as a process of improving. This is not something we learn one time like multiplication tables or algebra. Learning about stress is learning about life. There is no end of the semester when learning about life. What seems to work best is to deal with each stressor as an opportunity to gain new understanding and practice. The question is not how far we've come but what direction we are heading in.

If we learn from a stressful situation, we're moving toward improvement. As we keep that up, we get better and better. Over time we begin to realize that our lives seem more meaningful and satisfying. There is more peace and less tension. The hassles that do come up can be handled with more confidence. One or two weeks is usually enough time to start the process and recognize the value of keeping it moving in a positive direction.

Speaking from Experience

I didn't get involved in studying stress back in the mid-70's out of intellectual curiosity or because it seemed like a good career move. I became interested in stress because I wanted to survive. My basic nature is to be a high-stress person. I was a classic Type-A personality in my late 20's. A strong family history of heart disease and a nagging sense that life wasn't what it could be led me to begin learning about this topic. My goal was to learn and improve. This book is a summary of what has worked for me and the thousands of students, clients, and workshop participants with whom I've been honored to work with since the 1970's.

The approaches and skills that you will learn in this book are what I practice on a daily basis. They are what I teach to my students and clients. This is an ongoing process - every day there is something more to learn. It seems that the more we learn, the more we realize that each one of us is both insignificant and yet very precious. This book focuses on how we can began to improve in small ways that can lead to lasting progress in how we live and relate.

Organization

This book is organized in much the same way I teach workshops and classes, and incorporates much of the information I share with clients and students. It starts with general ideas and concepts and moves to more specific explanations, skills, and situations. The sequence is also similar to the treatment process that I have found to be consistently effective with clients.

Part One focuses on gaining a general understanding of what happens during stress. Chapters Two through Ten outline a model that I have been using in teaching and workshops since 1985. It describes the components of stress and illustrates how they interact. This involves a nuts-and-bolts explanation of how stress affects our body, mind, emotions, and spirituality. Part Two gets into specific approaches and techniques that allow us to restore a greater sense of ease and balance to our lives. Part Three introduces a set of principles that can be applied to stressful situations. I started using these principles around 1985. They grew out of years of reflection about the essence of what seemed to be effective when people made improvements in their lives. The ABC's described in Chapter Sixteen essentially summarize my practice when counseling or consulting. When I don't know what to do, I go back to the principles, and they always enable me to move things in a helpful direction. Chapter Seventeen looks at dealing with specific stressors such as work or relationships. Chapter Eighteen provides real-life examples (edited to protect the privacy of the individuals who lived them) of how students and clients have applied the information and principles to make improvements in their own lives.

Reading this book in order from start to finish will make the most sense, but I have tried to write it in such a way that you can skip around to get information that is immediately helpful and then go back and understand how and why it works.

Slow Down and Lighten Up

I would suggest that the first thing to do whenever you pick up this book is to read the title and then act on it. Slow down. Lighten up. If you can't do that, then turn to Chapters Eleven or Twelve, practice those exercises, and then pick up the book again. In my experience, it's a simple fact that we don't learn very well when we're tense or under immediate stress.

Please don't read this book in a hurry or when you have four hundred other things to take care of. (I would prefer that this book not become unfinished item number 401 in your life.) The best way to begin to make the most effective use of this material is to set aside the time and space to read, reflect and practice without tension or distraction.

Of course, if you could easily do that, you probably wouldn't be reading this. The point is that you don't have to be able to do it really well to get started. Just take a moment to begin moving in the direction of being more relaxed and more at ease. (Remember, if that seems hard to do, skip ahead to Chapters Eleven and Twelve).

Slow down, lighten up, and enjoy.

Part One

Understanding Stress

Chapter One

Stress is Bad for Us

Is There Good Stress?

That depends on whom you ask. Most books and workshops on stress talk about "good stress" and "bad stress"- "eustress" and "distress." These terms come from the work of Hans Selye, who was among the first researchers to study the effects of stress in depth. Dr. Selye came up with these descriptions to account for different reactions to "demands on the body" - his definition of stress.

The catch is that Dr. Selye's research focused primarily on physiological stress: he studied how our bodies adapt to physical demands. It is clear that some physical demands are not only good for us but necessary. Muscles lose tone and wither if we never use them. Lifting weights makes us stronger. These "demands" can be helpful.

The stress that we struggle with day-to-day is more than just physical. It also has mental, emotional, and spiritual components. I used the concepts of "eustress" and "distress" in classes and workshops I taught in the late 1970's and early 80's. I found that it was more confusing than helpful. Trying to sort out what is good and what is bad, how much is too much, and when and where there's not enough didn't seem to help bring greater ease and satisfaction to the lives and relationships of my students and clients. It is too easy to kid ourselves that we have the "right amount of stress" and then to add a little more.

The idea of "good" and "bad" stress seems to get in the way of dealing with day-to-day hassles and pressures in a healthy way. When most of us say the word "stress," we actually mean "distress."

In order to keep things simple and use words with commonly accepted meanings, I decided to set aside the concept of "good stress" and to use words like "excitement" or "challenge" instead. Dr. Selye pointed out that our body responds to challenge, excitement, or stress by increasing the flow of energy to our muscles. I believe that there is one very significant difference: what happens to that energy. During excitement and challenge the energy is discharged. The amount of energy that builds up matches what is released. This build-up and release of tension can actually lead to a relaxation response. We may be tired, but it is a "good" tired. Under stress the tension builds, but much, if not most, of it is not released. We're still tired, but it feels more like "worn out."

Wear and Tear on our Body, Mind, Emotions, and Spirit

Stress wears us out. It wears out our body, mind, emotions, and spirit. Tension is not something we carry around like an extra suitcase. It is an ongoing process of holding back energy that is flowing to our muscles. We are not aware of it because it is continuous. (Just as we aren't usually aware of wearing a ring we've had on our finger for years.) How this all works and what we can do about it are explained in more detail in Chapters Seven through Twelve.

Tension uses up our energy and puts pressure on our internal resources. Research over many years is pretty clear: our bodies don't fight off disease or recover from accidents or illnesses as well when we are under stress and tension. Our memory and problem-solving ability are diminished, our emotions more reactive, and our spirit deflated as stress levels increase. We don't feel as well. We don't perform as well, and we don't live as well as when we are able to prevent stress from taking over our lives.

Our body has a limited capacity to maintain high levels of tension. If stress and tension continue, something will break down. We may have emotional problems, headaches, back aches, or ulcers. We might have a stroke or heart attack. Stress can and does kill us. The bottom line is: if we don't manage stress, it will manage us.

Stress Limits our Flexibility and Receptivity

Invariably, when I say "Stress is bad" in a workshop, someone will say "But I work better under stress - sometimes that's the only way I get things done." That may be true, to some extent. This kind of stress usually involves a fear of consequences, as with a deadline that has negative repercussions if it's not met. Fear can be a powerful motivator. It can get us moving and keep us on task. However, I seriously question whether any of us can do our best work under stress. The problem is tension.

Tension limits our ability to take in information. It limits our ability to shift gears and to see things from a different perspective. It creates a pressure that takes away time to think, reflect, or look at the bigger picture.

We don't invest the time to listen thoroughly or to think things through before we act. Stress pushes us to get things done NOW while belittling us for not completing them sooner.

Tension makes us more impatient and reactive. Little hassles that we could easily let go if we were at ease become major events that can set us off or break us down. Stress-produced tension is essentially a waste of energy that distracts and diverts us from the task at hand. It takes extra energy to create and maintain tension, and it's no wonder that we feel tired and worn out much of the time.

Research has shown that people who have been awake for 19 hours or more perform at the same level as someone who is legally drunk. U.S. News and World Report describes a researcher at the National Institute of Mental Health who believes that "few adults in the industrialized world know the crystal-clear sensation of being completely rested" (Oct. 16, 2000). Many of us aren't aware of how worn out we are. Under long-term stress, we're so busy trying to keep up that we lose sight of our true gifts and potential. We need time to reflect, to see the whole picture, and to think outside the box in order to make intelligent, long-term choices.

Stress gears us up for action. It's called the "fight or flight response" for good reason. We don't smell the flowers or even see that we're stepping on them when we're running as fast as we can. When we're on the go all the time we don't have time to fully recover. When we're tired, we build more tension just to keep going; that puts us more out of touch and in trouble without even knowing it. We don't even recognize when we're becoming less effective.

Stress Diminishes Us

Stress is bad for us. By limiting our flexibility and receptivity, it limits our ability to understand ourselves, our situation, and others. Stress makes us more self-centered and impatient. It diminishes our efficiency and effectiveness, and can turn us into mindless robots stuck in a pinball-machine existence. Life is much more than bouncing off walls built of too many demands and too little time. Stress blinds us to life. There's no way to smell the flowers along the side of the road when we're going 80 miles per hour. Living fully does not mean filling up our days to overflowing. Living life to its fullest involves an appreciation and recognition that cannot be scheduled or organized. We need time and space to be ourselves. We need time and space to be with our families and loved ones. We need time and space to live.

Stress is bad for us. It limits our options and distorts our perceptions. It takes away our capacity for pleasure and our ability to love fully and deeply. Stress diminishes us. It turns us into something less than we could be.

Stress is bad for us. We need to understand it and learn how to undermine it. We need to learn how to find balance and make choices that enhance the health and well-being of our families and communities. This is not only possible, but not that difficult. That's what the rest of this book is about.

Chapter Two

Pieces of the Puzzle

The Obvious Components

If we think about the components of the stress response for a moment or so, three pieces become quickly apparent. First, there's a stressor - the source of stress. This would be where the stress starts. Situations like a disagreement at work, financial pressure, or too many things to do in too little time would be considered stressors.

A second obvious component of stress is that there is a person involved. People with different backgrounds and temperaments might be affected differently. But clearly we are an essential component of the stress puzzle.

The third obvious piece of the puzzle is that we have a response, or, in the case of someone already near their stress limit, a reaction. This response involves our body, mind, emotions, and spirit.

Stressor ⟶ Person ⟶ Response

Not-So-Obvious Component #1

The effect of a stressor on a person is not automatic. How a stressor affects us depends on how we perceive it.

I often use an exercise in my classes where students ask each other questions about their stress. In one class, two men who had similar backgrounds and work situations interviewed each other. One asked the other: "What is your greatest source of stress?" The second man replied: "Driving! I hate driving in heavy traffic, and since I work downtown, I do it every day. Sometimes I go to work early and come home late just to avoid the traffic." When he asked the first man "What do you do to relax?" the first man replied: "Driving. I love driving, especially in heavy traffic. I like to weave in and out, see if I can beat the flow." (He was probably one of the reasons the other man found driving so stressful.)

Here were two men, similar in many ways. Driving was a source of stress for one and a source of relaxation for the other. If we don't perceive something as a stressor, it doesn't lead to stress. I'll explain how and why this works in more detail in chapter four. I'll also argue that we have a great deal of control over how we perceive things and that we can actually learn to choose perceptions that serve us best.

Our puzzle now has four parts:

Stressor ⟶ *Perception* ⟶ *Person* ⟶ *Response*

Not-So-Obvious Component #2

Our response to perceiving a stressor is not necessarily automatic. It depends on whether we are aware of it. If we recognize a stressful situation, we can moderate our response and even prevent it from affecting our body, mind, emotions, and spirit. There are a number of skills and approaches we can learn that allow us to stop the build-up of stress once it starts and even eliminate the stress response altogether. These are explained in Chapters Eleven through Fifteen.

Making the Not-So-Obvious More Obvious

We can prevent stress to the extent that we are sensitive to the effects of perceptions and increasing tension. The problem is that increased stress decreases our sensitivity. The more stress we're under, the less likely that we'll be able to choose more effective ways of perceiving or responding to stressors. High stress is a lose-lose proposition. High stress levels wear us out and diminish our capacity to manage stress effectively. Less stress is win-win. We function better with less tension and are more able to recognize, reframe, and respond to potential stressors to the extent that we are already in balance.

The Whole Picture

Our stress model now has five components - three obvious ones and two that are more subtle. The subtle ones can be the most powerful once we understand and know how to work with them.

Stressor ⟶ Perception ⟶ Person
⟶ Awareness ⟶ Response

Unfortunately, stress doesn't just come in a straight line. It often comes from many directions at once, and our response to one stressor can generate a whole batch of new stressors. Things can get really messy. The rest of this book will focus on understanding how each part of the stress puzzle works and interacts while learning to separate and manage them effectively.

Chapter Three

Stressors: The Source

What's a Stressor?

A stressor is the beginning point of the stress response - the source of stress. It is usually an external event but not always. When I ask workshop participants to list their major sources of stress, the most common responses include: work, relationships, family, school, money, too much to do, health, boss, being a care giver, and dealing with kids, parents, neighbors, or day-to-day hassles. Dr. Selye defines stress as "a demand on the body." I find that his definition can help us to understand stressors, although I would add that the demands extend to our mind, emotions, and spirituality as well. We think of a demand as something that is urgent, something with an underlying threat or consequence behind it.

Threat or Consequence

My experience is that every stressor contains some kind of a threat, although it is often hidden or assumed. Stressors can threaten our security, our peace of mind, or our stability. They can threaten our livelihood, position, or possessions; our self-image, our standing, or our goals.

Some threats are up front and in our face, others seem to lurk in the background, tugging at us with a subtle sense of urgency that builds tension and pressure.

Sometimes the threats are not even real. We can often eliminate stress right at the source by clarifying the nature of the threat that pressures us. One example is indiscriminately striving for perfection. There are times when perfection is essential (brain surgery or airplane maintenance). On the other hand, there are also many more times when good enough is simply good enough. It's important to know the difference. For example, getting all A's is nice and may be necessary if your goal is to be accepted into Harvard Medical School. However, in many areas of work, the skills you develop and your attitude toward learning are more important than the grades you were awarded. If school is all we are doing, all A's may be a worthy goal and an effective challenge. But, if we are also working full time, raising a family, and being active in our community, pressuring ourselves to get all A's when there is really no threat if we get a few B's becomes one more stressor that we don't need.

Stressors Have a Context

Our reactions to previous stressors can be the parents of many new stressors. Hitting a traffic jam when we're late because of a heated argument with our spouse adds one more hassle to a pile that may already be near toppling over. Getting caught in traffic when we have lots of time and are pretty relaxed can be an opportunity for some quiet thinking time or a chance to finish listening to a book on tape. What may put us over our limit in one situation can be a minor hassle or even a welcome opportunity at another time and place.

Stressors often have momentum that drives our reaction before we realize what hit us. Slowing down enough to clarify the nature of the threat and the context that sustains our stressors allows us to separate ourselves from them and defuse the tension that can follow automatically. Parts Two and Three outline this process in more detail.

Getting Stressors Under Control

The concept of control seems to play a significant role in how much a stressor affects us. Participants in a research study were divided into two groups of roughly equal ability. Both groups were given a task that had been designed so it could not be completed. One group was given the illusion that actions they took made somewhat of a difference, but they still could not complete the assigned task correctly. When stress levels for both groups were measured, the group that had the illusion of control had a significantly lower stress response than the group that felt that their efforts made no difference.

Other studies looked at people who suffered from back pain that had a clearly identifiable physical cause. They were given a device they could operate that supposedly would reduce their pain but actually was designed to have no effect. A significant number of participants reported reduced pain.

In both cases, the illusion of control had a significant impact. If we think of control as always getting our way, we will pretty much always be under stress. However, if we think of control as being able to have influence or choices, we always have some level of control. Our options may be reduced to the lesser of two evils, but recognizing and making a conscious choice can reduce our stress levels enough to allow us to see other options more clearly.

There was a woman who walked in late to one of my classes, sat down in a huff, and said, so everybody could hear: "This is going to be a waste of my time." I stopped and asked what she meant. She said: "I'm only here because my counselor made me come. There's nothing you or anybody else can do for my stress." Upon further questioning, she told us she was a single mother with 5 children who worked full time in a dead-end job as the only support for her family. She was going to school full-time to be able to build a better future and was caring for her dying mother.

I asked her "Which one of those is most important?" She became impatient and said: "They're all important! There's no one else to take care of my kids. I have to work to survive. I'll have no future if I don't go to school, and I'm the only one willing to take care of my mother." I told her I recognized that each one of those things was very important, but, I asked, if she had to separate them, which might be a little more important than the others? There was a long silence as she stopped to think. Then she said in a quiet, almost tearful voice: "My mother - my mother is most important. She has only a few months to live, and I want this to be quality time for us. But it's not. I get so worn out, I get impatient with her and have even yelled at her a couple of times."

I heard from her a few weeks after the class ended. She hadn't given up her kids, her job, her classes, or caring for her mother but she was doing better. She had recognized how out-of-balance she had become and that she needed a break in order to focus on her mother in the way she wanted. She found someone to take care of the kids and brought her mother to her brother's house telling him: "You have to take care of mom this weekend." He told her he couldn't because he had a golf tournament. She said; "You apparently didn't hear me - you

HAVE to take care of mom this weekend"; and she left to take care of herself.

She got some rest, practiced the exercises described in this book, began getting more sleep, and made some minor changes in her schedule and priorities. It was enough to make a significant difference in her relationship with her mother, and, she had discovered a new-found assertiveness that she hadn't realized she was capable of. She was in control because she recognized she had choices.

Clients, students, and workshop participants often tell me they are "between a rock and a hard place." Clarifying the nature of the rock and the hard place while making simple choices about priorities gets things moving in a new direction.

One man told me that he started dreading going to work when he first woke up in the morning. His boss was 30 years younger than he, was nowhere near as competent, and did everything he could to make the older employee miserable. This student was one year away from retirement (the reason that he wasn't promoted to his boss's position) and said: "I can't handle this job anymore and I can't quit because I'll lose my retirement - I'm between a rock and a hard place."

Again, the simple question: "What's most important." This was followed by an impatient answer ("Both!"), and then careful thought. Finally he said: "My retirement is most important. We've been building a cabin on a lake and it's almost done. I wouldn't give that up for anything." Weeks later, I received some feedback. He had started being less tense at work. When he was hassled, he thought about fishing in front of his new cabin. As he relaxed, his boss seemed to back off. Later he realized how much pressure he had been putting on his boss by questioning his knowledge and experience. They never became close friends, but they were able to work together without escalating stress levels.

When we perceive that we have control, stress is reduced. It is important to remember that we always have some control. Our lives become easier to the extent that we recognize and make choices that move us in a healthier direction.

We face a wide range of demands in life. They become stressors because we see or feel some sort of underlying threat within them. We can significantly reduce the impact of these stressors in our lives when we clarify the nature of the threat and take time to recognize and act on our choices and priorities.

Chapter Four

Perception: All the Difference in the World

What Really Is Reality?

Sometimes when our thoughts or ideas seem a little far out, someone will tell us to "Get real." We assume that there is a single, universal reality and that if someone doesn't agree with our assumption, they need to "get with the picture." However, anyone who has played with photography knows that how you take a picture makes all the difference in the world. What we see depends on how we look at it.

There is simply no such thing as pure objectivity in relationships. We can't clearly observe something that we are a part of. And it's even harder for an outsider to determine the "reality" of a relationship. Our behavior will change when we know we're being watched. Anyone we do not know who watches us without our knowledge will miss gestures and tones that have personal meaning. If they do know us well, observations will be prejudiced by this previous knowledge. How we view our relationships sets firm limits on what they can become. This doesn't mean that simply convincing myself that a conflict is resolved means that everything will be fine. However, believing that it can be resolved is a necessary step toward resolution. Most, if not all, of our stress is touched by human relationships. Since there is no objective reality about relationships, there is none about our stress either.

Edward deBono, in his 1990 book "I Am Right, You are Wrong" (Viking Press, New York, 1990), contrasts "relationship thinking" with objective thinking in a fine metaphor in which he distinguishes between "rock logic" and "water logic." I have adapted these concepts to materials that are readily at hand when I am teaching a class or workshop.

Objective thinking ("rock logic") involves objects such as a pen. I keep a pen in my briefcase and take it with me wherever I am working. It has been in a number of different cities and states, in cars, and on trains and airplanes. It's there whenever I need it; it hasn't changed except that some of the ink is used. I often borrow a couple of pens from workshop participants and mix them with my pen. I can still pull my pen out and it still has not changed. A pen is an object. It will stay basically the same no matter where it is or what is it mixed with.

Working with objects is much simpler than dealing with people. There is consistency and logic and, in most cases, it is possible eventually to figure out exactly what's happening. Relationships and stress are not like that. Relationships and stress are more like water. When water is in a pitcher, it takes the shape of the pitcher. If I pour it into a glass, it takes the shape of the glass. Its shape depends on where it is. That's more like us. Right now we are different from when we first opened our eyes this morning. We are different than at the happiest moment of our lives. We're different than at the most difficult moment of our lives. How we respond depends on where we are and where we've been.

If I pour some hot coffee into cold water, I create a new liquid - weak lukewarm coffee water. I can't get my hot coffee back. I can't get my cold water back. They have changed. That's more how people operate. We are changed by other persons if we are open to them. If we are not open to them, we are changed by the process of closing ourselves to them.

Relationships and stress are fluid and changing. They depend on where we are, where we've been, and how we see things. These are choices. If we slow down enough to reflect on our options, we can choose both our perceptions and response.

Perceptions Can Lock Us Up

I once worked with a man who had been locked in seclusion for thirty years. He had been tied up in restraints almost continuously for three years. Whenever he was let free, he would violently attack whoever was near by.

This was in the 1970's. Our state had just developed a new mental health code and it became illegal to keep someone tied up all the time. This man had been transferred to the facility where I happened to be working because we had a small Psychiatric Unit and the facility where he resided had requested an evaluation. I was asked to consult because I had a lot of experience working with people with a history of violent behavior.

The program director had four of the biggest, strongest attendants bring him into the building, but this new resident still put out three hallway windows with his foot on the way to his room. When I came to visit, I opened the door to his room, stepped in just far enough so that I was closer to the door than he was to me, and stood in an open, relaxed, non-threatening stance that I had found to be effective with others who were acting out. He was pacing back and forth across the other end of the room. I started talking to him but he did not respond.

I noticed that he had an incredible amount of tension in his neck and forehead, and guessed that he must have a splitting headache. I told him that I knew something about headaches and tension and that maybe I could help him get some relief from his headache. Asking him to sit on his bed, I told him that I would try some relaxation approaches. When he sat, it was the first sign that he understand language. He did not respond to my treatment, but he tolerated it without a problem. I sat down next to him and talked a little more, but he never responded or looked at me.

When I got up to walk out, I saw that there was a crowd looking through the small window in the door. As I left, the nurse who had coordinated his admission and knew his history said: "I don't believe it. He attacks everybody. He has never not attacked anyone." One of the onlookers was a new staff person, quite young, who had just finished his training. He said "That's nothing" and walked into the room, talked to the man, and also was not attacked.

This new, inexperienced staff person put his finger exactly on what worked - "nothing." For thirty years, every time this man had human contact, people approached him expecting a fight. He gave it to them. Usually more than they could handle. Then, twice in one day, two people came in with nothing - not expecting a fight. He didn't fight.

This man stayed at our facility about a month. The new staff person was assigned to work with him one-on-one. About a year later, I happened to visit the facility where this man lived. He was back in the seclusion room, but they had taken the lock off and he could come and go as he pleased. Changing perceptions changed his life.

The Brain That Organizes Itself

The human brain is described as a self-organizing system. Rather than being pre-programmed, it organizes itself according to its owner's experience. Again, I am indebted to Edward deBono ("I Am Right, You are Wrong") for the metaphor that I use to describe how our perceptions are formed: In some ways, our brain is like my neighbor's back yard. There was a sand pit on the back of his property when he bought the place - basically a hill with a big hole where half of it had been hauled away. One weekend he used a bulldozer to make a smaller hill with a nice gentle slope. When it rained on what was then a smooth hill of sand, the rain ran down the slope and formed a number of little rivers. When it next rained, the water did not form new rivers but found its way down the ones that had formed previously. Winter came. When the snow melted, it too went down the same gullies formed previously.

Our perceptions work like the rain and snow on that smooth sandy hill. We have an experience that is registered in our brain as a series of connections. When we have a similar experience, the same connections are likely to be made. I have found that stress increases the speed of the "rivers" in our brain. We are more likely to automatically interpret something based on previous experience to the extent that we are more stressed.

The key here is to learn to see where our "rivers" are taking us and make new ones when the old ones don't fit where we want to go. We can recognize patterns of perceptions that work and those that don't. We can learn

to choose to view stressful situations in ways that lead to
health and fulfillment rather than in ways that lead to
stress and hassle. This is not a quick and easy process,
but it can be accomplished with some effort and a commitment to maintaining a balanced life.

Learning to Choose

A number of years ago I got a referral from another
therapist to work with a couple that he had been seeing
for some time. He told me that he was unable to get a
handle on what was happening with them. When he
tried to sort out a recent conflict, their portrayal of the
event was so different that he had to make sure that they
were describing the same incident. They also had some
very destructive patterns of behavior. Over many years,
each had learned the other's buttons and sore spots and
could set them off at will. There were a number of situations that always resulted in a big argument - riding in
the same car, going shopping together, and - the worst
- deciding what to do on holidays.

After working with the couple for a short while, I got
an image in my mind that I shared with them. I said:
"You seem to be like a couple of dueling microscopes.
Each of you looks at the other from such a very narrow
point of view that they don't even intersect." Over the
next few sessions, we worked out mutually acceptable
agreements on some current issues about budgeting and
child care. Then, at the end of one session, the wife said:
"I never expected us to get along this well. This is good
enough for me. I don't want to mess with success. This
is my last session." Her husband said: "I want to continue. I want us to grow closer, to share our lives more,
to be intimate." She said: "Go for it. I'm outa here."

The husband continued in treatment and became

very interested in the idea of perceptions. At one point, he made a decision that he was going to view his wife differently. He decided that he would try to see his wife through compassionate eyes rather than defensively as he had in the past. Of course he failed the first time they had an argument. But he kept on trying and learned from each mistake. After a number of months, Thanksgiving came and went without an argument. Christmas followed - no argument. (His wife called it the miracle of Christmas.) They went shopping together after the holidays - no argument. They took a trip to Texas together. Three full days in the same car - no argument. They began going on "dates" and were enjoying each other's company when we decided to end treatment.

This man had little evidence on which to base this change in perception. He simply made a decision and chose, again, and again, and again, to follow through with it. It changed his behavior toward his wife, and eventually she couldn't hold on to her old perceptions of him. Their relationship and their lives changed.

We can't simply snap our fingers and decide that everything is different. Clarifying our perceptions is a skill that requires understanding and practice. Parts Two and Three will describe how we can do this in more detail.

Chapter Five

Person: How Much Can We Take

That's Us

We are the middle component in this stress model. Stressors are perceived by people. We may or may not be aware of how tension is building in our body, mind, emotions, and spirit, but we react to it. Stress, as I understand it, is a human creation. I don't see examples of the kind of stress we experience among animals in nature. Part One of this book focuses on understanding the components of stress: stressors, perceptions, awareness and reactions. This chapter asks the question "What can we do about us?"

Limited Capacity To Adapt

I believe that there are limits to what we can do about us. A lot of stress-management programs emphasize regular exercise, improved diet, and generally paying closer attention to our health as an effective way to deal with stress. These things are very important for overall well-being and disease prevention. But they serve more as a temporary relief from symptoms of stress than as an effective way to manage and prevent the stress response.

I have worked with college and professional athletes as well as a lot of patients and students who exercised on a regular basis and took good care of their health but still suffered from stress disorders.

I think that placing a high value on diet and exercise does increase our ability to endure stress to a certain extent, but there appears to be a definite limit to levels of tension that we can successfully adapt to. We can increase this limit a bit, but the limit is still there and it is very easy to exceed it even if we are taking good care of our health.

Weak Link

Stress creates tension which causes wear and tear on our body, mind, emotions, and spirit. If we keep it up, something will eventually wear out. That's when things start to break down. Each of us has a weak link - a price we pay when stress levels go too high for too long. It may be back pain, digestive problems, anxiety, headache, or emotional problems. It could be a heart attack or stroke. Our weak link is often something that drastically changes (or ends) our life.

If we drive our car on a track at top speed continuously, something will break down. Most cars are designed to be operated near the speed limit - they are not built for running at top speed all the time. Neither are we. Our bodies and minds are not put together in such a way that we can endure intense stress over the long term. Something will break down.

What We Can Do

Parts Two and Three outline specific strategies and principles for preventing and managing stress. In general, I have found that stress becomes less of a problem in our lives to the extent that we establish habits of improving. Life looks different when we realize that we are headed in a positive direction. Feeling stuck becomes a temporary inconvenience rather than a life-long trap.

I worked as a psychologist at a residential facility for developmentally disabled people in the mid to late 1970's. I was assigned to a unit with 26 profoundly or severely retarded men who had problems with impulse control and violent behavior. They spent their day in a large room with very little equipment or furniture - things were broken so often, it made little sense to replace them. About thirty to thirty-five times a week, on average, staff would have to physically hold someone down to stop them from hurting someone or breaking up the place.

The facility director, Dr. Marlin Roll, challenged me to come up with a program to deal with this problem, and he added a very interesting directive. He said: "Don't focus on trying to stop them from acting out. Ask yourself what do you want them to do?" I talked with staff to see what might be possible, and their response was that there was virtually no time to do anything. Most of these residents needed help with basic tasks like eating, dressing and shaving. By the time staff breaks were figured in, there was only about an hour and a half of free time on the morning shift and about the same during the afternoon shift.

I pulled together some materials from the closets and ordered a few things and began spending time with each of the residents to find out what they could do. I took out some blocks and figured out how many blocks each one could stack. I did the same with puzzles, throwing and catching a ball, and other similar tasks. The staff agreed to run a program for the hour and a half each shift, five days per week. (Weekends were busy with additional duties.)

We divided the room into areas with different activities in each area. Staff were given a simple assignment: "help them improve." If the form indicated that Joe could stack three blocks, teach him to stack four. If Fred could throw a ball five feet, work with him on throwing it seven feet. If Henry could put a two-piece puzzle together, give him a three-piece puzzle.

A number of the residents were highly volatile. One person escaped from the locked unit one day and did $3000 worth of damage in fifteen minutes. Some did not know their names. Hardly any could talk. One resident had a maximum attention span for activities of about fifteen seconds. We worked with him fifteen seconds at a time.

Within three weeks of starting the program, there was an 83% decrease in disruptive behavior. We went from over thirty major disruptive incidents per week to three to five per week. There were fewer incidents on midnights and weekends when they didn't run the program. The only change we made was a regular opportunity to improve.

A few months later, staff approached me with a request to take four of the residents who had among the most violent histories to a Christmas store where there were thousands of very fragile Christmas ornaments on display. I supported their request, and there were no problems. The residents were fascinated by the display, and nothing was damaged.

Regular, ongoing improvement changes how we view our stressor and ourselves. It leads to lasting improvement in our lives and relationships.

Chapter Six

Awareness: Knowing When to Stop

Signs of Stress

Parts Two and Three of this book describe a number of exercises and approaches that have been consistently effective in reducing and eliminating the effects of the stress response. These techniques work only if we are aware of when to use them. The key is learning to recognize increasing stress levels sooner rather than later. There are a number of indicators of stress that we can learn to pay attention to. Some appear to be universal. Others will be unique to each person.

Habits and Patterns

It is helpful to spend some time debriefing ourselves after a stressful time. When did we first notice that our stress levels were going up? How did we become aware of that? What were some specific signs that things were getting worse? At what point did everything seem to fall apart? Were there any indications that this was going to happen?

Investing even ten to fifteen minutes in this exercise can give us some really useful information. The answers can vary a lot. Some of us may recognize that we start moving faster as stress increases. Others may notice they are eating more often. We may recognize an irritability, or shortness of temper. Maybe we feel more tired and less motivated.

If these or any other responses seem to pop up each time we begin to get stressed out, they can be an indicator that it is time to do something about it. All of the approaches in Parts Two and Three work faster and more effectively when our stress levels are more short-term. The longer our stress builds, the longer it takes to recover. Chapters Seven and Eight explain the physical reasons behind this.

Catching our Breath

One of the responses to stress that we all share is a change in our breathing. Stress breathing will tend to be faster and/or shallower than relaxed breathing. (Of course, if we never relax, we won't notice the difference.) Chapter Eleven focuses on using our breath to undermine the stress response. As you practice this approach, you'll began to notice signs of stress in your breathing earlier in the stress response.

Tension and Stress

Whenever there is stress, there will be tension. (For details on how and why this works, see Chapters Seven and Eight.) Each of us has a unique pattern of tension in our body that builds up in response to stress. Some of us will feel it in our neck, others in our shoulders, still others in our legs, head, or back. There is a common pattern to this tension that is very helpful to recognize. We all tense up. This is a literal term. The muscle groups that pull up from the ground in standing or sitting are active during the stress response.

Every time we tense a muscle group, there is an opposing muscle group that must relax. If I bend my arm, the muscles on the front of my arm are doing the work, and the muscles on the back must let go. When I straighten my arm, the muscles in the back pull my hand down while the muscles in front let go. During the stress response, the muscles that pull up from the ground tense. We become "uptight." You never hear of someone becoming "down-tight." We literally "tense up." No one ever "tenses down." These words describe what is actually happening.

I have found that more muscle groups become involved as stress levels increase. Our whole body tenses up at once when we are under a lot of stress. This is a well-established pattern that has been evident in every client, student, and workshop participant I have worked with since the mid-1970s.

There is a simple way to break the pattern, and this seems to consistently inhibit the stress response as well. When we press down with our feet or stand with our knees bent and our weight centered, we began to become aware of how we are tensing and can let go. The details of this approach, called grounding, are described in Chapter Twelve.

I worked on-call for a number of years and had to respond to a wide range of mental-health emergencies. One afternoon I got a call that a woman was having a severe panic attack and that I needed to go to her home. I understand a panic attack to be a self-escalating pattern of physical, mental, and emotional tension that spirals out of control. When I got to the woman's home, the ambulance was there, ready to take her to the hospital. She was sitting in a chair gasping for breath and could not communicate. Her whole body was almost lifting off the chair from the tension. I asked her daughter to press down on her mother's knees and push her feet toward the ground. After about five minutes, the woman could communicate. I talked her through a breathing pattern that undermined the stress response. Fifteen minutes later, the ambulance left without her. She was all right.

We can't tense up and tense down at the same time. If we push down or use the grounding stance, we stop tensing up. We also begin to feel how our body is tensing. Once we are aware we are tensing, we can stop. Our individual patterns of tension become more and more evident as we use this approach. Once they begin to resolve, we can notice even small increases in tension. Then we know that we have the option to act and stop the stress response in its tracks.

Anticipating and Preventing

As we work with these approaches, we will begin to notice subtle increases in tension or changes in our breathing when we even think about a potentially stressful event. We will also more readily recognize situations that have resulted in high stress in the past. Preventing stress is always easier than trying to manage it in the moment. Being able to anticipate and prevent stress allows us to maintain a sense of ease and balance in potentially difficult situations. We solve problems instead of being victimized by them.

Chapter Seven

Reaction: My Nerves Are Shot

All of Us

We react to stress with our whole self. Body, mind, emotions, and spirit are all affected by stress and are targets for management and prevention. The next four chapters, along with Part Two, look at these aspects of ourselves separately, but it is important to remember that each of us is a whole person. We cannot separate our body from our mind or our spirituality from our emotions. These are parts of us that function together as a single whole. We separate them only in order to make them easier to study and understand.

Our Body Under Stress

Stress is often described as the "fight or flight response." This pretty well sums up what happens to the bodies of both humans and animals under stress. When an animal is threatened, it will either fight or run away. Its body becomes charged up and ready for action. This is an adaptive response that often saves its life.

Human bodies also become charged up and ready for action during the stress response. The difference is that fighting or running away does not solve most human problems and most likely they would make things worse. Animals discharge the build-up of energy in their muscles through physical action in response to stress. We have learned to hold back this impulse. That is how tension is produced.

People who suffer from long-term stress often say "My nerves are shot." That's actually a pretty good description of what happens to our body in response to long-term or intense stress. The stress response starts with the nervous system. To be more specific, it starts with the autonomic nervous system, which contains the nerves that regulate where energy goes in our body. (My description of this process may be a bit oversimplified. The intent is not to present a detailed description of physiological concepts but simply to understand that which we want to learn to regulate.)

Our autonomic nervous system is made up of two parts which function in opposition to each other. The sympathetic nervous system is connected to our muscles - it energizes them when we need to act. The parasympathetic nervous system is connected to our internal organs. It regulates body-maintenance functions such as digesting food, fighting off disease, keeping our blood clean, etc.. In a healthy individual, these two parts of the autonomic nervous system alternate in a balanced way to allow our body to adapt to the needs of a given situation.

The stress response always activates the sympathetic nervous system. This sends energy to the muscles, getting us ready for action. When the sympathetic nervous system is activated, the parasympathetic nervous system is suppressed. As one is turned up, the other is turned down.

A simple way to undermine the stress response is to stimulate the parasympathetic nervous system. Since the stress response requires sympathetic nervous system activation, stimulating the parasympathetic nervous system prevents the energy from going to the muscles and thus prevents tension from building. I have seen this be consistently helpful in stopping the build-up of tension since the early 1970's with several thousand people (including me). We stop the stress response when we activate the parasympathetic nervous system. There is no delay; the process takes less than a minute. As soon as the parasympathetic system begins to dominate, the stress response loses its power. (The specific techniques that accomplish this are described in Chapter Eleven.)

That doesn't mean that we are suddenly free of stress and tension. We still need to recover from the tension that has built up. This recovery can occur quickly with short-term stress. If our nervous system is in good balance when we begin to experience a stressful event, we can recover in less than a minute once the parasympathetic nervous system is stimulated. However, if the stressful event is particularly intense, or if our stress levels have persisted or increased over hours, days, months, or, sometimes, even years, recovery gets more complicated.

Over 1,400 physical and chemical changes can take place in our body in response to long-term stress. Essentially, everything in our body shifts focus so that maximum energy is sent to the muscles. An animal whose life is threatened in the wild shuts down all non-essential functions in order to focus all its energy on running or fighting. Civilized humans have learned to restrain this impulse. Holding back this extra energy results in more built-up tension, which, rather than being adaptive, interferes with our ability to handle the situation.

Our body adapts to long-term high stress by producing stress hormones, which allow the sympathetic nervous system to continue to send energy to the muscles even though we are exhausted. Stimulating the parasympathetic nervous system suppresses the energy going to the sympathetic nervous system and stops the build-up of stress. This can make a significant difference in how we respond to the situation, but it does not take away the tension that may have been escalating for months. The stress hormones need to be cleaned out of our blood before we can restore a more natural sense of balance to our nervous system and our lives. Our liver is prepared to do this cleaning, BUT, it needs to be activated by the parasympathetic nervous system to work properly.

This is accomplished by stimulating the parasympathetic nervous system on a regular basis over time. My experience is that doing this six times per day for three to five minutes over a period of two to four weeks is sufficient to get us back into balance in most situations.

There seems to be a point where we begin to become much more reactive as our stress levels increase. I call it the sunburn line. (My guess is that it corresponds to a certain concentration of stress hormones in our blood, though I have seen no research on the point.) It is very helpful to get to know our sunburn line. When we're below the line, new stressors will temporarily increase our tension levels, but we recover fairly quickly. When we're above the line, even a little stressor can send us off the charts. It's just like having a really bad sunburn - even a light touch can make us yelp with pain. If there were no sunburn, a hard slap in the same place might hurt a little bit for a short while. We get to know our sunburn line as we approach and cross it and by becoming more aware of tension in the body. (See Chapter Six.) We can learn to recognize a level of tension that begins to feel like sunburn and then to take action and make decisions that prevent us from going over the line.

Learning to regulate our parasympathetic nervous system gives us the ability to stop tension from building in the moment and to recover from accumulated tension over time. The feedback I've had on this approach has been very consistent. People who have tried this method report handling a wide range of stressful situations much more effectively. When they practice these balancing techniques over time, they report an increased sense of ease and satisfaction in their lives.

Chapter Eight

Reaction: My Mind Is Spinning

How Stress Affects Our Mind

Stress affects our mental functioning in four inter-related ways: 1) Our focus becomes more narrow; 2) We become less receptive, less able to take in new information; 3) It becomes harder for us to concentrate; and, 4) We tend to recycle or repeat negative thoughts over and over.

Narrowing focus is an adaptive response for an animal who is threatened. A few years ago I woke in the middle of the night to the sound of glass breaking. I ran outside and saw that some of our chickens had flown through the window of the chicken coop. I grabbed the pitchfork and opened the door to see a silver fox sitting in the laying boxes, eating the eggs. I jabbed the pitchfork in front of the laying boxes and the fox quickly moved back and forth between the two boxes. Whenever the fox moved, I moved the pitchfork in response. I (along with the pitch fork) became the total focus for the fox. It didn't glance over at the remaining chickens to see which one might make a good meal. It kept its entire focus on the guy who could cause serious damage with the pitch fork. Fortunately for the fox, I was struggling with myself about using that pitchfork. It was a beautiful animal, yet if I didn't kill it, there was little question that it would be back and my chickens would disappear. I must have moved a second too late while I was having this internal dialogue, because the next thing I saw was a silver blur whizzing out the door.

Maintaining that singular focus under a threat saved the fox's life. The problem with human stress is that our threats are much more complicated and rarely come from a single direction. Most often we are dealing with multiple stressors as well as memories from past stress. As we narrow our focus, we miss other things that are happening. In many cases, the solutions to our problems and stress lie hidden among those other things.

Stress gears us up for action mentally as well as physically. We easily get so caught up in what we are doing (or should be doing) that there is no space for contemplation or reflection. I recall a lesson learned when installing a ceiling fan when we were building our home. I had workers scheduled to help finish drywall early that next morning and needed the fan to circulate the heat from the wood stove so that the plaster would cure properly. Upon coming home from work, with an evening meeting scheduled shortly after dinner, I thought "If I hurry, I can get this up before the meeting." I hurried and got it up and running. But after the meeting I noticed that I had hung the fan directly over the stove. A call to my neighbor confirmed that the fan had to be moved: the heat from the stove would ruin the fan. There were lots of unforeseen complications with the new location but, though tired and frustrated, I persevered until well after midnight and got the fan up and working.

The next day, my wife looked at the fan and said: "Why did you hang it there?" She couldn't understand why I had put the fan in such a strange place. It was because of a typical mental response to stress. My first focus was to get the fan up and working. The second focus was to move it a certain distance from the stove. I never took the time to ask myself: "Where would be a good place to hang this fan?" The fan came down one more time and was moved to the center of the room where it is now both attractive and functional.

Hurry and pressure limit our vision and receptivity. We can get stuck on one track and totally miss that there might be other influences or considerations. When we struggle with numbers of stressors at the same time, our focus gets pulled from one to another. We are dealing with one problem but thinking about what needs to be done about two or three others. The result is distraction and difficulty concentrating.

Mind and Body

Our mind and our body are intimately connected. When we think about something our body gets ready to perform. When our mind and body are both focused in the same direction, there is little stress. We are generating energy but using it toward a productive end. However, when our mind is scanning all of our various stressors or dwelling on old hassles, stress and tension increase.

When tension is building, our mind is drawn to focus on "what's wrong?". Dwelling on stressors creates more tension and a greater tendency for our mind to be distracted. Our thinking becomes less and less productive as tension and distraction escalate. Long after a stressful event has passed, the escalating tension continues to pull our thoughts in a negative direction. We repeat similar thoughts again and again. This recycling of our thoughts continues to build stress and tension until it seems that our minds just won't stop. The same stressful events can be recycled through the night and into the next day when we return to the stressful situation with even fewer mental resources to deal with it effectively.

The simplistic solution is to tell ourselves "Don't think about it." I have never found this to work. Trying not to think about something draws our thoughts right back where we don't want them. Chapter Thirteen outlines specific exercises that teach us to take control of our thoughts, to let go of unproductive thinking, and to focus on solving the problems at hand. These are not difficult skills to learn; and most clients and students report improvements within a week or two. However, these skills become much more effective to the extent that we practice them regularly and maintain overall balance with our body, mind, emotions, and spirit.

Chapter Nine

Reaction: Emotional Sunburn

What Are Emotions?

I have found emotions to be among the most misunderstood human experiences. Some of us have been told that emotions are something to be avoided - a sign of weakness. Others have heard that emotions are a way "to get in touch with ourselves," that somehow they define who we are. Some of us have been told to control our emotions, others to express them fully. A person who is "emotional" is often thought of as being unstable. Yet an "emotional experience" can imply something deep and meaningful. One who is "in touch" with his or her emotions is described as being more "real" and "down to earth." Yet if we make decisions based on emotions, we are thought to be irrational and irresponsible. We describe emotions as "feelings," yet they are thought to be mental experiences - we seek "mental health" services to get help in dealing with emotional problems.

My training and experience have led me to understand emotions as our body's response to our perceptions of the moment. There are three characteristics of emotion that are important to remember: 1) Emotions are primarily physical events - they take place in the body. 2) Emotions are a response to perceptions - what we focus on and how we view it will determine our emotional response. 3) Emotions are temporary, momentary experiences.

When we experience an emotion, there is movement in our muscles. It is literally a "moving" experience. With training, it is possible to observe this movement. It is also possible to measure it with the appropriate equipment. We literally "feel" our emotions in our bodies. This relationship links emotions to the stress response. Since emotions affect our muscles, and the stress response activates the musculature, stress will have a tendency to amplify our emotional experiences. Experiencing an emotion when we are in balance may be pleasant or unpleasant, but it is not necessarily stressful. However, if we are under stress, the build-up of tension gives more power to the emotion than our perception of the situation would normally arouse. I call this the "sunburn response." Increased tension can also block the experience of emotion leading to a feeling of being numb or empty. We either become more emotionally reactive or numb under stress.

Emotions always have a context. There is something that we are perceiving or thinking about that stimulates an emotion. Emotions quickly change when our perceptions and thoughts change.

The observation that emotions are momentary requires some explanation. You can say that it can take us months or years to "recover" from the loss of a loved one. Isn't this an ongoing emotional experience? Yes, but it is not one single emotion. This experience consists of hundreds or thousands of thoughts, memories, and experiences that stimulate similar emotions. I experienced deep sadness when my parents died. There were a lot of experiences that brought this loss to mind shortly after their death. Contact with friends and family, planning and participating in the funeral services, going to their house when they were no longer there. These and other experiences stimulated my sadness. Shortly after each of them died there were hundreds of reminders that they were gone. They had been a regular part of my life and then suddenly were no longer there. As time went on, there were fewer reminders and therefore less sadness. Now when I think of them, it's usually a happy memory and it brings a smile to my face.

Emotions move (e - motion). Experiencing emotions is a normal part of daily life. If we acknowledge the emotion and allow ourselves to fully experience it, it passes. Thinking about the situation that stimulated the emotion will precipitate a new emotion. The stressful pattern of recycling our thoughts described in Chapter Eight can create a series of emotional responses that keeps us in turmoil.

We create emotional tension when we don't acknowledge and experience an emotion. We often try to stop feeling something because it is too unpleasant or because we have heard from someone that we're "not supposed to feel that way." Seeing emotions as a weakness creates the same problem. It has to do with how we try to stop feeling. Since emotions involve movements in the musculature, we can stop this movement by tensing our muscles. Think of a young child who has been told to "stop crying." She will tense her chest and neck, hold her breath, and shut her jaw. She stops crying - it works. The problem is that it also builds tension. If we do not release this tension it simply adds to the stress response as well as increasing numbness and/or reactivity.

Crying is simply a mechanism that helps the body release emotional tension. Trying to stop crying builds tension. I have often seen clients who cry even though they are trying to hold it back. This is like pouring water in a glass while you are emptying it. There can be a net gain of tension through this process. If we simply accept and experience emotions, they pass and are gone. To the extent that we hold them in, they create more tension, which intensifies both the stress response and our emotional reactivity.

There was a common belief in the 1960's and early 70's that we needed to express all of our emotions. This depends on the situation. There are many situations where expressing our emotions could interfere with our effectiveness in dealing with the problems at hand and others where it might be inappropriate and lead to increased stress. Chapter Fourteen will focus on how to deal with emotions in a healthy way. For now, I will simply say that we can experience an emotion without expressing it outwardly. How and if we choose express that emotion is an entirely different question that depends on the situation and those involved.

Chapter Ten

Reaction: Spiritual Deadening

A Part of Life

I recently added our spiritual reaction to the stress model. Doing so was not an attempt to proselytize or advertise my own beliefs. It is simply a recognition that the spiritual component is a vital part of our lives. Our spirituality can take many different forms; some may choose not to acknowledge it at all. But my experience is that spirituality is both affected by stress and a vehicle for effectively managing and preventing the stress response. I have observed over many years that clients who have a strong spiritual commitment seem to recover and put their lives together more quickly than those who do not.

I use a very broad definition of spirituality in applying the term to this model: spirituality is that which affects our spirit and determines our overall relationship with the world. I believe that spirituality contains our belief about the purpose of our lives and our place in the world. In many ways, it is our understanding of who we really are. Although I acknowledge that there are those who may not believe in God, I use the name "God" to refer to the moral authority and focus of spiritual development in our lives.

Stress and Spirit

Stress affects our spirituality in a number of ways. First of all, it leads to numbness, a lack of feeling about spiritual issues. This effect makes sense since stress diminishes our receptivity. We become less aware of and sensitive to the role of God in our lives when we are under stress. Spirituality challenges us to take a stand when the world confronts us with a challenge to our beliefs and values. Stress and tension either keep us moving too fast to take a stand or wear us out so much that we don't have the energy to stand up for what is important to us.

We become less aware of our spiritual side as stress levels increase. Spirituality easily slips into the background, crowded out by increasing demands and pressure. Our attempts to gain spiritual nourishment under stress may result in a sense of dryness or emptiness that further confirms the fact that we are moving away from God. This spiritual desert is not always a result of stress. It is also a well-described aspect of the spiritual path that helps us to deepen our faith and humility. We can respond to spiritual deserts by reaffirming our commitment and direction and continuing to move toward God. If we seem totally stuck and immovable, then we have at least the choice of looking toward God and accepting that where we are may be a necessary resting place on our journey. This process will be discussed in more detail in Chapter Fifteen.

Tension Leaves Room for Little Else

The second way that our spirituality is affected by stress involves tension. Developing our spiritual side requires sensitivity and reflection, time and patience. Tension pushes these aside by increasing our reactivity and sense of pressure. Spirituality challenges us to deepen our understanding of ourselves and our world. Tension creates a wall that keeps us sliding along at the surface of things. Spiritual experiences embrace the moment. Time slows as we realize the continuity and relationship of all things. Stress and tension create too much momentum for us to fully experience a given moment. The deeper meaning of our experience becomes a blur that fades into the background as we rush off to meet another demand.

Spirituality and Relationships

Spirituality is really about relationship. It encompasses both our relationship with God and with each other. All major religions have love and compassion at their core. Stress undermines love by making us more self-centered. This can take many forms: we can become more controlling; our egos may begin to push concern for others aside; we may become totally immersed in our pain; or it might seem that we just don't care anymore. The extreme form of this is suicide, which is really the most self-centered action possible. Our focus on our pain becomes so all-encompassing that we fail to see the value of life itself.

A brief review of major religious beliefs makes it clear that God does not want us to be frazzled. Virtually all religions value peace and serenity. The greatest saints and spiritual masters were not high-stress people. On the contrary, they were people who found an inner harmony that overflowed into the world so that they became models for the rest of us. We also can aspire to realize our full potential, but we must recognize that stress is a major obstacle to spiritual development.

Part Two

Restoring and Maintaining Balance

Chapter Eleven

Getting Our Nerves in Balance

Regulating Tension

Restoring and maintaining physical balance involves learning how to prevent the build-up of tension in our bodies. Chapter Six pointed out patterns of tension that correspond to the stress response, while Chapter Seven described how tension is produced when our autonomic nervous system gets out of balance. The next two chapters focus on developing specific skills that allow us to arrest and prevent the build-up of physical tension.

The build-up of tension in our muscles interferes with almost everything we do. It inhibits smooth movement and wastes energy in addition to blocking receptivity and clear thinking. In athletes, tension interferes with performance and increases the likelihood of injury. There is no build-up of surplus tension when there is a balance between energy and action. Getting rid of built-up tension allows us to function at full capacity and effectively adapt and respond to changing circumstances.

I think of tension as a process rather than a static condition. Instead of thinking of tension as something we "have" or "carry," it helps to recognize that tension is something that we are doing as well as something that has built-up from what we did in the past.

When we stop tensing, we begin to relax. The key is to recognize how and when we are tensing, to learn ways to stop it and then to set up regular practice in order to recover from tension that built up over time.   I will describe two methods for doing this. This chapter explains the process of Natural Rhythmic Breathing, which allows us to regulate our autonomic nervous system.[1]   Chapter Twelve describes a process called "grounding" which helps us become aware of patterns of built-up tension in our bodies and helps us learn to let them go.

Undermining Tension at the Source

Chapter Seven explained how the two parts (sympathetic and parasympathetic) of the nervous system work in opposition to each other. Stimulating the parasympathetic nervous system suppresses the sympathetic nervous system, which supplies the energy that creates tension. We can stimulate the parasympathetic nervous system by changing the way we breathe. Specifically, it involves movement of the diaphragm, which is a muscle, shaped like a parachute, at the bottom of our lungs. When this muscle moves up and down in a slow, steady, continuous rhythm, the build-up of tension stops. This does not immediately resolve tension that has built up over time, but it does stop tension from building in the moment.

I have seen this effect in thousands of people over the past four decades. When the diaphragm is moving in a slow, easy rhythm, it ends the build-up of tension. My understanding is that the slow, rhythmic movement of the diaphragm stimulates the right vagus nerve, which passes through the diaphragm and is a primary compo-

---

[1] Previously, I referred to this as "Diaphragmatic Breathing." I stopped using that term because many others use it to teach a wide range of techniques that are quite different from this process.

nent of the parasympathetic nervous system. This movement needs to be fairly precise to be effective. It doesn't work when there are stops and starts or pauses. It doesn't work when it is too fast or too slow.

How to Feel Your Diaphragm

A simple way to feel your diaphragm is to gently press the palm of your hand just below your sternum (breast bone), where your ribs begin to separate. Sniff a few times, as if you were trying to get a whiff of a familiar smell on the wind. The bouncing that you feel under your hand results from the movement of your diaphragm.

How To Breathe Using the Diaphragm

The first time you try it, it is helpful to keep your hand below your sternum as described above. As you inhale, allow the air to come all the way to the bottom of your lungs - you will feel the diaphragm move. Once the diaphragm is moving, it can be helpful to put your hand over your abdomen, near your belt line. Your hand will move out as you inhale and in as you exhale. Allow this movement to settle into a slow easy rhythm. Allow three to four seconds for the inhale and the same for the exhale. Do not pause between breaths. Make sure that it is your breathing that is moving your abdomen, not your muscles. Pushing in and out with your abdominal muscles has no effect and will interfere with Natural Rhythmic Breathing.

It is easier to move the diaphragm if you are leaning back slightly. If you are leaning forward, your diaphragm presses against your stomach and intestines and this can restrict the movement a bit. A subtle but important part of mastering Natural Rhythmic Breathing is to think of allowing it to happen rather than making it happen. Trying too hard generates tension, which overrides the parasympathetic nervous system. Be patient. A bit of practice may be necessary to get it right, but it is well worth the effort.

When done properly, Natural Rhythmic Breathing immediately stops the stress response from building. You can feel a difference after three or four breaths. This can slow things down enough so that you can avoid saying or doing things that are likely to make a tense situation worse. Continuing to practice the Natural Rhythmic Breathing during a stress situation helps to clear our thinking and allows us to evaluate our options. In over forty years of working with Natural Rhythmic Breathing, I have never seen someone continue to build tension when their diaphragm is moving in the proper rhythm.

Things That Get in the Way

Occasionally, clients or students will report that Natural Rhythmic Breathing is "not working" for them. Over the years, I've identified a number of things that seem to subvert the effects of this process. The most common is when the breath starts in the chest before the diaphragm begins to move. It is necessary for the inhale to come all the way to bottom of the lungs. Think of filling a glass with water. The water goes to the bottom of the glass first and then fills the rest of the way. Our breathing needs to follow the same pattern in order to stimulate the parasympathetic nervous system.

Another common problem is breathing too fast or too slow. I have found that Natural Rhythmic Breathing works only when there is a minimum of three seconds and a not much more than four seconds for each inhale and exhale (for a total of six to eight seconds for each full breath). I am not sure why this is true, but it has been very consistent in my experience. I worked with a man who had a lung injury from breathing noxious chemicals. He was suffering from panic attacks, and I noticed that he was taking only about a second for each inhale and exhale. We used a stop-watch to train him to slow his breathing. The panic attacks stopped once he reached three seconds.

Pausing between breaths also seems to subvert the effects of Natural Rhythmic Breathing. Again, I am not sure of the reasons for this, but my experience has been consistent. Stress symptoms begin to disappear when the inhale and the exhale are continuous without any pause between them.

A more subtle way to undermine the effect of Natural Rhythmic Breathing is trying too hard. It can appear that someone's abdomen is moving up and down in a nice, easy rhythm when actually it is being forced by effort, thus creating tension and stimulating the sympathetic nervous system. The effort of forced breathing is usually evidenced by a furrowing of the brow or tensing of the jaw. It seems that when the autonomic nervous system gets contradictory messages, the sympathetic system wins and overrides the parasympathetic response. It is not necessary to breathe perfectly the first time you try it. But it's helpful to remember that Natural Rhythmic Breathing is your body's natural way to breathe when you are at rest. Our bodies want to breathe that way. We simply have to pay attention and allow it to happen.

Sometimes there appears to be a significant amount of tension in the diaphragm and you simply cannot seem to get the diaphragm to move. I have seen this particularly in working with clients suffering from chronic pain. In most cases, continuing to practice the Natural Rhythmic Breathing (without trying too hard) eventually loosens things up enough so that it has the desired effect. Occasionally, using other relaxation approaches can settle things down enough to allow the diaphragm to began moving effectively.

What if I Can't Do It?

I have discovered some tricks that appear to help stimulate Natural Rhythmic Breathing when it seems difficult. I have also used these approaches with children and mentally impaired people who weren't able to understand verbal directions. The simplest technique is to lie prone (on the stomach) with a pillow under the chest. This restricts chest breathing enough so that the air moves down to the diaphragm. It usually takes a little longer this way than when we can start the process consciously, but I have found it to work well. A similar technique is to hold a pillow, or just our arms, gently against our upper chest. .

We can often stimulate Natural Rhythmic Breathing by making a very full exhalation - breathing out all of our air until the lungs feel empty. Then we simply relax. The next breath most often will move the diaphragm. I would recommend not doing this more than once, to avoid hyperventilation. Another technique is to press very gently against the abdomen during the exhale and then to lift your hand during the inhale. This seems to stimulate the Natural Rhythmic Breathing.

Breathing Patterns During Stress and Activity

It's not possible to use Natural Rhythmic Breathing when we are physically active. We use our chest muscles to breathe when we need extra oxygen to support activity. We can feel our chest heave in and out whenever we engage in strenuous activity. Breathing this way stimulates the sympathetic nervous system and is the type of breathing that is evident during the stress response. Chest breathing is the opposite of Natural Rhythmic Breathing. It is also the "normal" mode of breathing for someone who struggling with long-term stress. Clients and students will sometimes start out using a blended kind of breathing when first learning this technique. The abdomen clearly moves, indicating that the diaphragm is working, but the chest also moves. It makes a difference which moves first. I have found that there is eventually a positive effect if the abdomen rises first, indicating that the diaphragm has moved first. However, in my experience, if the chest moves first there is no effect. After regular practice, when the breathing becomes natural, the chest does not move at all.

Remembering to Use It

The hardest thing about learning to control the stress response through Natural Rhythmic Breathing is establishing the pattern and remembering to use it. We breathe all the time, and we're not used to thinking about how we breathe. Clients and students who are most successful set up a routine in which they link practicing Natural Rhythmic Breathing with a normal activity in their daily schedule. Some like to practice when they first wake up; others after their morning shower or before breakfast. Linking Natural Rhythmic Breathing with meals is a good practice, because stimulating the parasympathetic nervous system helps with proper digestion. Other popular times include during normal breaks, while driving, in the elevator, during commercials, while waiting, and before going to bed. Natural Rhythmic Breathing can be very helpful if one has trouble falling asleep. Sympathetic nervous system activation interferes with sleep. Stimulating the parasympathetic nervous system turns down the "nervous" energy that can keep us awake.

How Often and How Long to Practice

The amount of practice that has seemed to be consistently effective in restoring balance, in my experience, is six times per day for three to five minutes. Many have reported significant progress by practicing less. However, no one I have worked with has remained in a high-stress state after practicing Natural Rhythmic Breathing six times per day for two to four weeks. Most people report that after consciously practicing for three or four weeks they notice they are moving the diaphragm in the proper rhythm without thinking about it. That's an indication that your body is regaining its physical balance.

Regular practice leads to the condition where Natural Rhythmic Breathing becomes your normal pattern of breathing during rest. It is still helpful to continue practicing at regular intervals, but many report that they automatically begin breathing in the natural rhythm at times when previously they would have practiced, such as at meals or before bedtime. When Natural Rhythmic Breathing becomes a regular part of our lives, there is a tendency to notice when our breathing changes in response to increased stress levels. We now have a very helpful indicator that not only helps us recognize potential stressors but also cues when to practice Natural Rhythmic Breathing in order to stop tension from building before it really gets going.

Chapter Twelve

Recognizing and Releasing Physical Tension

Patterns of Tension

Each of us has a unique pattern of physical tension that builds up as a result of the stress response. The first step in letting go of that tension is learning to recognize it. This chapter describes specific exercises and techniques that help us to identify and release tension that comes from stress. The key is in recognizing how we tense up under stress and then reversing that pattern so that we undermine the stress response.

Chapter Six described a common pattern of tension that we all share when we experience stress. We literally "tense up." Muscles that pull up and away from the ground are activated in response to stress. I have noticed that, as tension increases, muscles tend to work more in groups. It becomes more difficult to move individual muscles separately when there is more tension. When we are under a lot of tension, our whole body responds in a consistent pattern. I've learned that disrupting the overall pattern of tension helps us become aware that we are tensing other groups of muscles, and we are able to stop the build-up of tension throughout our body. We

Figure 1
Standing with tension

disrupt this pattern of tension by putting ourselves in a position that interferes with tensing up. We can do this by pressing down with our feet while sitting or standing in a way that makes it impossible for us to tense up our whole body. This technique is called grounding.

Figure 1 illustrates what, for most of us, is a normal upright standing posture. However, there is actually quite a bit of tension that is being generated to maintain this position. The legs are straight with the knees locked, the shoulders and chest are lifted slightly, and there is tension all along the spine. Although this may look normal to the untrained eye, there is a considerable amount of tension being generated simply to maintain this position. These tension patterns become exaggerated during the stress response. Bending our knees disrupts this pattern of tension. We begin to feel how we are tensing when our knees are bent. The same thing happens when we are sitting and press our feet into the ground.

What Is Grounding?

"Grounding" is a term that was originated by Alexander Lowen, who founded Bioenergetics, an approach to psychotherapy that integrates mind and body. When we are grounded, we are aligned so that our bones support us with a minimum of effort from our muscles. The muscles of our legs must work to hold us up when our knees are locked. Bending our knees slightly releases this tension and gives us more flexibility. It also disrupts the pattern of tension that is part of the stress response.

Variations on the grounding position are common in sports and martial arts. Body tension will distort a golfer's swing, a karate master's kick, or a baseball player's throw. All of these motions must be carried out with the knees bent if they are to bring about the desired result. Standing with our knees bent and our weight centered behind the balls of our feet is a balanced position that allows us to move with the greatest ease in any direction.

Grounding helps us become aware of and in touch with our body. It also has mental and emotional effects. Grounding "puts our feet on the ground" both literally and figuratively. We think of someone with their "feet on the ground" as being stable, solid, and clear-headed, with common sense and a good grasp of what is realistic and possible. The physical act of grounding has the psychological effect of "putting our feet on the ground." We think and see more clearly when we are grounded. We become more aware of our surroundings and more in touch with the feelings and concerns of those around us. This fact makes sense when we realize that our body is the vehicle through which we relate to the world. Any restriction of our physical awareness will restrict the information that is available to us.

Our mind can go anywhere. We can be thinking about the dinosaur age, and a second later shift our thoughts to what life might be like in the year 3000. Even though it carries the effects of our past experiences, our body exists only in the present time. Being in touch with our body puts us in touch with what is happening right now. There is no stress when we are fully absorbed in what we are doing at the moment. When mind and body come together in the activity of the moment, stress disappears. That's why hobbies that absorb our full attention, such as woodcarving or flower arranging, are so relaxing. Our body produces exactly the amount of energy that is needed to carry out the task our mind is focused on. No excess tension is produced. The mental exercises described in the next chapter become much easier to practice after doing the grounding exercises described below.

I have worked with a number of people who have been diagnosed with dissociative disorders. Their attention easily splits away from what they doing at the moment, and they can easily lose track of what they are doing or where they are going. This is not uncommon among people who are suffering from post-traumatic stress. I recall trying to talk with a woman who struggled to answer simple questions because her attention would fly off in one direction or another. I finally stopped the interview and taught her grounding. She became more able to focus as she stood in the grounding position and we were able to finish the initial interview. A few weeks later, after consistently practicing grounding, she was able to be productive again, and to make plans and follow through with them.

Our language reflects how being grounded influences behavior. People are not grounded when they get "upset," or when they "act up," or "blow up." We become grounded as we "slow down" and "settle down." A man who had been separated from his wife because of an abusive incident told me "I use the grounding and breathing as soon as I start to feel upset. It settles me down and I can listen to what she's saying. Before, I would blow up and not even realize what I was doing, let alone what she was trying to tell me."

Thoughts About the Grounding Stance

The correct grounding stance is a precise alignment of our body with the forces of gravity. However, this precision is not the most important aspect of grounding. Grounding is helpful to the extent we are moving in the direction of becoming more grounded. Being exactly in balance with our body structure and the forces of gravity gives us a center point that we can move toward. It is not a position to be held rigidly - using tension to achieve grounding defeats the whole purpose of the exercise.

Most people initially report that the grounding stance is uncomfortable. That is to be expected for a couple of reasons. First, it's not the usual way of standing for most people and so can feel a bit awkward. Second, grounding helps us to become aware of tension in our body and we will experience this tension as discomfort. However, it is important to distinguish discomfort from pain. Grounding is a process of working *with* our body rather than *on* our body. Pain is the body's way of telling us something is wrong. Even though we commonly hear the phrase "no pain, no gain," pain is not "gain" when doing these exercises. We often tense in response to pain and thereby undermine the positive effects of grounding.

It is helpful to differentiate between the grounding exercise and the grounding stance. In the grounding exercise described below, we bend our knees deeper and pay close attention to our overall posture. The grounding stance simply involves bending our knees slightly and adjusting our weight so we feel it just behind the balls of our feet. It is helpful to use the grounding stance any time we are standing up. We can significantly minimize the amount of tension we build in our bodies to the extent this becomes our normal way of standing.

It is also important to maintain Natural Rhythmic Breathing throughout all of these exercises. You don't want to be creating tension when you are working to become aware of it and to let it go. Chapters Seven and Eleven describe how Natural Rhythmic Breathing helps us to stop the build-up of tension that results from the stress response.

How to Practice Grounding

1. Start with your feet. Place them about the width of your hips apart. If this feels unstable, move your feet a little farther apart. Align them pointing straight ahead so that if you were to draw lines from your heel to middle toe on both feet, those lines would be parallel. Figure 2 illustrates the proper position. (You might feel a bit pigeon-toed in this position since many of us tend to stand with our feet pointed outward.)

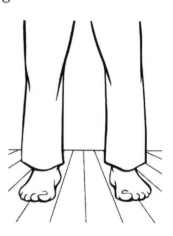

Figure 2
Proper position of feet
for grounding

2. Gradually allow your knees to come forward as your pelvis moves back. Shift your weight until you feel that it is centered just behind the balls of your feet. One way to test this is to lift your heels slightly. If you lose your balance, your weight is back toward your heels. Figure 3 demonstrates the proper grounding stance. The vertical line illustrates how the alignment is consistent with

Figure 3
Proper grounding stance

the force of gravity. The pelvis is supported by the legs, which are bent at the knee and flexible. The spine is supported by the pelvis and the head by the spine. The top of the head is directly over a point just behind the balls of the feet.

Figure 4 illustrates a common distortion of the grounding position. Many people tend to tilt their pelvis forward when they bend their knees. Notice that the line drawn down from the top of the head comes down behind the heels. Increased tension is necessary to maintain the position in figure 4, while the position in figure 3 minimizes tension. It is helpful to use a mirror to guide our positioning when learning this exercise. The key is to have our pelvis back and our weight centered just behind the balls of the feet. One way to feel this is to gently shift your weight from your toes to your heels and gradually find the centered point.

This may feel a bit awkward at first. A lot of people report that they feel as though they are going to fall forward when they assume the proper grounding stance. That simply means that their habitual way of standing incorporates a pattern of tension that shifts their weight back on their heels.

Figure 4
Pelvis forward

Grounding Exercises

Simply standing in the grounding stance is a very effective exercise. Your legs might start to shake after you maintain this position for a while. That's simply an indication that tension is being released; it is a normal part of the grounding process. If it becomes uncomfortable, bending your knees a little less will reduce the intensity. Remember that the purpose of these exercises is body awareness. Trying to push yourself to go past discomfort is counterproductive.

As you work on relaxing into the grounding stance, you will begin to notice patterns of tension as areas of discomfort in your body. You can begin to release this tension through gentle stretching or slow, easy movement. Tension involves holding. Movement and stretching are the opposite of holding and tend to relieve built-up tension. It is important to remember the terms "gentle" and "slow" when doing these exercises. Fast movement or extreme stretching can easily damage a muscle that has held a lot of tension.

A very helpful exercise that can be done from the grounding stance is to very gently bounce downward. This involves rhythmically flexing our knees as we let our shoulders, arms, neck, and jaw relax. Chapter Six described how various muscle groups work in opposition to each other. The stress response uses muscles that pull up and away from the ground; bouncing downward involves the opposing muscles. We cannot tense up and bounce down at the same time.

Another helpful grounding exercise is to let your head drop forward and gradually roll down until your hands touch the floor or you reach a point of discomfort. Your legs maintain the grounding stance as you bend at the waist as shown in Figure 5. It is important to breathe

Figure 5
Hanging over grounding
exercise

Figure 6
Improper head position

slowly and deeply during this exercise and to focus on
relaxing as you exhale. Note that your knees remain bent
throughout the exercise. It is also important to be aware
of the position of your head. There is a strong tendency
to raise your head so that you are looking at your feet
or the floor (Figure 6). This creates tension in the neck
and shoulders that needs to be avoided. You should be
able to see the wall behind you from this position. If
your eyes look toward your feet, there is tension in your
neck. How far down you are able to go with your hands
is a function of your overall body flexibility and has no
impact upon the effectiveness of the exercise. Simply go
down as far as is comfortable.

There is no set amount of time to maintain this position except to stay within your comfort levels. A minute
or so can have a significant calming influence. If you
come up too quickly from this position you are likely to
become light-headed. It is best to slowly roll upward
from the base of your spine while continuing to allow
your head to hang. Think of starting from the bottom
of your spine and gradually setting each vertebra on top
of the one below it. Figures 7, 8, and 9 illustrate this

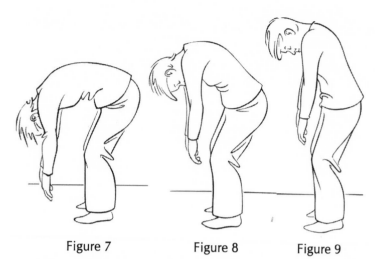

Figure 7   Figure 8   Figure 9

sequence. Slowly breathing in as you rise, and relaxing during the exhalation, prevents light-headedness and helps to further relax the muscles of your back, neck, and shoulders. Grounding is not a position of relaxation when we are first learning it. It is more likely to feel awkward and uncomfortable. As we become more familiar with it, however, we gradually let go of tension that restricts our efforts. After a time, it becomes very relaxing, and we realize that we feel more comfortable, and move and work with a greater sense of ease, to the extent that we are grounded.

Chapter Thirteen

Recovering Mental Balance

Learning to Control Thoughts

Thoughts can be both a source and a result of stress. Thinking about stressful events can create as much tension as experiencing those events in the first place. Our mind is drawn to stressful thinking as tension levels increase. Chapter Four described how our brain works as a self-organizing system: Our view of reality is based on previous experience and perception. How and what we think determines our view of the world and the people who live here. Chapter Eight explained how our mind reacts to stress by narrowing our focus; how our thoughts influence our stress and tension levels; and how the mental recycling of negative thoughts can send our stress levels spiraling. This chapter describes how to let go of stressful thinking while finding ways to bring resolution to our problems and a sense of ease to our thoughts and activities.

Thoughts tend to drift into our mind at random when we are not focused. We can jump from one train of thought to another without realizing where our mind has been or where it is taking us. The exercises in this chapter help us to make choices about how we think and what we think about. The first step is to break up destructive habits of thinking; the second is to learn to focus in ways that help us to resolve our problems and accomplish our goals. Three techniques will be described. The first, which I call "Thought Refocusing," provides a way to let go of harmful habits of thinking.[2] The second technique, Meditation, helps us learn to let go of unwanted thoughts and to focus where we choose. The third technique, which I simply call "Clarifying," helps us to recognize where our thoughts are leading us and to see a larger picture and relevant details more clearly. Using each of these techniques makes it easier to use the others to build an overall strategy for recovering and maintaining mental balance.

Thought Refocusing

Thought Refocusing provides a way out of the mental recycling of negative thoughts that often follow stressful events. Long after the incident has passed, we persist in repeating thoughts such as "How could he do that to me? ... What right does she have to say that? ... Who does he think he is? ... Why does everything happen to me? etc." These thoughts create tension and interfere with clear thinking and problem solving. Trying to push unhelpful thoughts out of our minds sounds easy but never seems to work. We might stop thinking about them for a few seconds, but the thoughts return again and again.

It is helpful to recall the metaphor used in Chapter Four which compares our brain to a sandy hill and habits of thinking to the little rivers that are formed as water runs down the hill. The trenches become deeper as more water runs down the hill. New water is more likely to run down the deeper trenches. Repeated thoughts create connections in our brain which make it more likely that

---

[2] I previously used the term thought focusing.

those thoughts will be repeated again. Thought Refocusing creates "another river" on the sandy hill that is our brain. Deepening this "river" through repetition makes it easier for new thoughts to go in that direction.

Thought Refocusing involves choosing a "Rhythm Phrase" that brings you a sense of peace and hope and can be repeated in rhythm with breath or activity. It can be a short prayer, a quotation, part of a poem, or any saying that brings you a sense of peace and hope. I have found that the length does make a difference. When observing clients practice this technique, I notice that their breathing doesn't have as smooth or easy a rhythm with phrases that cannot be effortlessly repeated within six to twelve seconds.

Examples of Rhythm Phrases that I have used include: "Love is patient, love is kind"; "Guide our feet in the path of peace"; "Rooted and grounded in love"; "Peace and Calm (repeated very slowly) and my favorite "Always choose love." It is helpful to take some time to choose a phrase that has particular meaning to you and that fits the situation at hand. It's best to stay with one phrase at first so it becomes more quickly established in your brain.

Once you have chosen a Rhythm Phrase, start to repeat it silently to yourself whenever you have mental "down time" - while driving, taking a shower, going for a walk, waiting in line, doing household chores. Its not hard to find time for hundreds of repetitions per day. Repeating the phrase sets an easy rhythm and brings a sense of peace to these activities, but, more important, it establishes a deeper set of connections (or "rivers") in your mind. Starting to recite your phrase as soon as you realize that you are recycling disruptive thoughts allows you to let go of negative thoughts and restore your peace of mind.

Most people report that they are able to successfully replace negative thinking with their chosen phrases after less than a week of practice. It can be particularly helpful to use Thought Refocusing when stressful thoughts interfere with sleep. It is also beneficial to link repetition of the phrase with Natural Rhythmic Breathing whenever possible. Simply repeat the first half of the phrase during the inhale and the second half during the exhale.

What Is Meditation?

The term "meditation" has been used to describe a wide range of practices including reflection on a single topic, prayer, and guided imagery as well as a variety of relaxation techniques. The meditation I teach is much simpler than all of those and has been practiced for thousands of years. A considerable amount of research indicates that it reduces muscle tension, lowers blood pressure, and stimulates brain waves associated with deep states of relaxation. People who practice meditation regularly report that they feel calmer, more rested, more peaceful. These are good reasons to consider learning to meditate, but, in my experience, one of the most important benefits is that it teaches us to control our thinking. Meditation helps us recognize when our thoughts are taking us in an unhelpful direction and allows us to choose how and what we think.

In some ways, our mind is like a radio that we can't shut off - it is always thinking about or commenting on something. Learning to focus our thoughts on what is relevant at the moment allows our body to relax and take care of itself.

Meditation involves centering our attention on a single focus and gradually letting go of any distractions that come up. When we are able to maintain this focus, we experience an increased sense of calm, peace, and relaxation. However, distractions are part of the process and eventually we realize that we are thinking about something else. That is where the mental-skill-building aspect of meditation comes into play. We simply allow the distracting thought to pass and gently return our mind to the single focus. This can happen dozens or even hundreds of times during each meditation session. Meditation trains our mind and our brain to let go of distracting thoughts and return our focus where we choose. Trying to push away distractions or force our concentration interferes with this process. Effective meditation requires no effort or experience. It is simply a process of gently letting go of whatever distractions arise and returning our attention to the focus of the meditation.

I personally have found this to be an invaluable skill not only in managing and preventing stress but also in problem solving and communicating with others. The regular practice of meditation helps us learn to suspend one way of thinking and look at a person or situation in new ways. It develops the capacity to let go of self-centered or unhelpful thoughts and listen more fully to what others are saying. This became clear to me during a particularly high-stress time in my life. Since I had been meditating for a number of years, it had become part of my daily routine. I continued meditating during this difficult time, but experienced constant distractions during my regular meditation. I found that after a short while, my ability to control the focus of my thoughts in my work and while under stress had significantly improved. My meditations during this time were not particularly peaceful or satisfying, but they accomplished for me what I needed at the time.

There is no such thing as a "bad" or unproductive meditation. If we stay with our focus, we feel relaxed and refreshed. If we have lots of distractions, we get lots of practice in letting go of unwanted thoughts and choosing our focus. In most sessions, we get a bit of both. Meditation is a process of developing and fine-tuning a skill. The key is regular practice. A professional basketball player will shoot many thousands of baskets before making it to the pros. If a player stops practicing for a while, she will get "rusty" and need work to bring back the earlier skill level.

Meditation becomes most effective when practiced on a regular basis. I've been practicing it regularly since 1972 and when I skip a day, it feels like the mental equivalent of not brushing my teeth. My thinking is just not as clear or astute as when I meditate daily. I find that I am even more creative and productive on days when I am able to meditate two or three times. Meditating more than three times per day does not seem to make any difference.

When to Meditate

It is most helpful to find a regular time when you can meditate every day. It is more important to meditate regularly than to meditate for long periods of time. Practicing five minutes once per day will be helpful. Ten minutes will be much more helpful and twenty or thirty minutes is significantly more helpful than that. Likewise, once per day is helpful, yet twice or three times are even more helpful. In my experience, practicing more than thirty minutes or three times per day does not seem to bring much additional benefit. The important thing is to work out a regular routine that can work with your schedule and commitments. You may decide to increase the time once you begin to experience the benefits. The key, however, is regular practice.

Choosing a Meditation Technique

Most religions and martial arts disciplines teach forms of meditation. Some people have tried to make up their own meditations, but I have found these to be less effective than techniques that have stood the test of time. If you are using a form of meditation that was learned from a well-trained, experienced instructor, I would encourage you to continue that. Changing your meditation technique tends to interfere with the learning process, and I would suggest not altering your meditation practice without good reason. I will present two options for meditation in this book. One is over 2500 years old and comes from Yoga; the other is a Christian prayer, called Centering Prayer that has been practiced for over 1800 years.

How to Meditate

It is helpful to follow a set routine when learning to meditate. Following the same steps each time makes it easier to settle into the process. Setting aside a regular time and place for meditation helps us to be oriented and prepared for the practice. Sitting upright in a relaxed position with our feet on the floor is the best position for meditation. Since meditation is done with our eyes closed, it is too easy to fall asleep if we meditate lying down and too difficult to fully relax if we are standing. It is important to begin the meditation with Natural Rhythmic Breathing and then use a technique that helps to focus our attention.

Paying attention to the sensation of your breath at the tip your nose serves this function. You will notice that your breath feels cooler as you inhale and warmer as you exhale. Focusing on that physical sensation helps to ease you into the meditation process.

The next step is to silently repeat a sound with each inhale and exhale. If you want to practice the yoga meditation, use the sound "so" on the inhale and "hum" on the exhale. These are Sanskrit words that mean "this" and "that." To incorporate the Christian Centering Prayer into your meditation, simply repeat the name "Jesus" with each breath. Slowly say the first syllable with the inhale and the second syllable with the exhale. Continue repeating the sound until the time you have set aside for meditating has passed. (You can either set a timer or check your watch or a clock to see when you are finished.) When distractions come into your mind, simply let them pass and very gently return your focus to your breathing and repeating the sound. Do not try to force your concentration. Remember that distractions are a natural occurrence and not an indication that you are doing anything wrong.

Clarifying

If we picture our thoughts as a line on a piece of paper, high stress turns straight lines into circles and scribbles. Stress seems either to drive our thoughts over and over the same issues or to bounce them from problem to problem. Nothing gets resolved, and we feel increasingly worn out and frazzled. "Clarifying" is a method of straightening out our thoughts by focusing in a productive direction. It is also one of the three principles of stress management that will be described in much more detail in Chapter Sixteen.

A lot of our stressful ruminating takes the form of questions: "What happens if I lose my job? What if I can't pay that bill? What if we don't make it on time?" Clarifying involves answering these questions and asking others that help us get a clearer picture of our priorities and options. A student described an incident where he was running late for work. He was becoming more and more agitated as new obstacles (some the result of his increasing tension) made him even later. He described the following process as he was driving to work: "I started doing the Natural Rhythmic Breathing and settled down a bit. When I got stuck in traffic I realized there was nothing I could do to get there faster and decided to try to clarify my thinking. What would happen if I was late? Well, if I tried to sneak in and pretend I was there on time, I could get caught and my boss would be really mad. If I simply came in and told her I was late, she would be less upset. Actually, I am hardly ever late. I got to work, went to my boss's office, and apologized for being late. She looked up and said 'no problem" and didn't give it a second thought. I started working and had a really good day. Later on, my boss came up and told me she appreciated my honesty."

Clarifying involves asking and answering good questions. It straightens out our mental circles and scribbles and takes them in a positive direction. It helps us accept what we can't change, see what choices we have, and realize what is most important. We create a lot of stress worrying about things that never happen. Worrying creates extra tension that only interferes with our ability to deal with stuff that does happen. Clarifying helps prepare us for the worst-case scenario. It turns worrying into problem-solving. There is no tension when our mind is focused on dealing with a single issue. Tension builds when we recycle stressors or split our focus. Clarifying prevents the build-up of tension and helps us see the path that works best for us.

Stressful thinking can also involve going over and over past hurts or injustices. Clarifying in these situations can either help us find resolution or lead us to other techniques that can untangle our thinking. One example was a client who was deeply distressed by an injustice and couldn't sleep because she kept going over and over it in her mind. Clarifying helped her step back from her gnarled thoughts and recognize there was nothing she could do about the situation while lying in bed trying to sleep. She said: "I told myself that thinking this was just making me more upset and then started using my Rhythm Phrase phrase along with the Natural Rhythmic Breathing. I fell asleep and didn't wake up until the alarm went off."

We further clarified the situation that had kept her awake by asking "What could you have done differently?" She said she wouldn't have done anything differently; her actions had interfered with someone else's political ambitions and they had taken steps to reduce her effectiveness. Other questions followed: "How important was the stand you took? What are the long-term consequences of what happened? What can be done to correct the situation after the fact? What would it cost in terms of time and effort? What is the likelihood you would succeed?" Answering these questions and asking other related questions helped her to reach a decision. Once the decision was made, she was able to stop ruminating and carry out her plan.

Clarifying frees us from mental entanglement by separating issues and looking at them one at a time. It not only stops the build-up of tension from mental stress but re-directs our focus in ways that lead to acceptance and resolution of our difficulties.

Chapter Fourteen

Maintaining Emotional Balance

A Healthy Emotional Response

Chapter Nine explained the nature of emotions and how they are affected by the stress response. Emotions are simply part of the human experience. They are natural events that take place in our bodies - we literally "feel" our emotions. The first step in a healthy emotional response is to acknowledge and accept what we are feeling and to allow ourselves to experience that emotion. The second step is to clarify the emotion and make a decision how best to proceed. This chapter describes the process of acknowledging, accepting, and clarifying emotions without building up additional tension that contributes to the stress response.

Letting Go of Tension

Emotions pass naturally if we do not interfere with them. Unfortunately, many of us try to stop our emotions because they either make us uncomfortable or interfere with a mistaken belief that emotion is a sign of weakness. We stop feeling by tensing our muscles and holding our breath. We are often not aware of this response to emo-

tion because it is such a long-standing habit. Letting go
of the tension allows emotion to run its course. Emotions
can make us cry either if there is a certain level of intensity to the situation or if there is a build-up of tension
from holding back previous emotion. Crying is a natural mechanism for releasing emotional tension. Trying
to stop ourselves from crying creates additional tension,
which interferes with maintaining emotional balance.

Natural Rhythmic Breathing (described in Chapter
Eleven) and grounding (described in Chapter Twelve)
are both very helpful in helping us deal with emotion in
a healthy way. Natural Rhythmic Breathing stops tension from building up; grounding helps us to be more
aware of our body and how we might be tensing in response to our emotional experience. The most common
pattern of tension when someone is trying to avoid an
emotional experience involves tensing the chest, raising
the shoulders, holding the jaw closed and furrowing the
forehead. Taking a few slow breaths, pressing our feet
into the ground, and letting those muscles relax allows
the feeling to pass.

Accept and Acknowledge

Allowing ourselves to breathe and relax during an
emotional experience requires us to accept and acknowledge our emotions. If we believe we "shouldn't be feeling this way," we will tend to create tension that will
inhibit the emotion. Emotions appear to be controlled
not by the logical, rational part of our brain (the cerebral
cortex) but by a much more primitive area called the lim-
bic system. This means that emotions are not necessarily
logical. I have never found it helpful to try to explain
"why" someone is feeling something, although it is helpful to understand and clarify "how" they are affected by

their experience. Reminding ourselves that emotions are normal experiences, while recognizing that they can be uncomfortable but are temporary, allows us to relax and tolerate them.

It can also be helpful to identify or name the emotion. Finding the word that best describes what we are feeling makes it easier to connect with that emotion. It is very common for a client to be on the edge of tears and then finally let go when they find the right word to describe what they are feeling. This establishes the connection which helps them let go of the resistance. The emotion is freed to move on and does so.

Distinguishing Thoughts and Sensations from Emotions

It is easy to confuse emotions with thoughts and sensations because of the language we use in describing these experiences. For example, saying "I feel like going outside" is not a description of an emotion. I may be thinking about going outside or I may have a sense that some fresh air or exercise would be good for me right now, but these are sensations and thoughts rather than emotional experiences. Likewise, saying "I feel that this is right" is also not an emotional statement. It is rather a thought or judgment. We may sense or think that something fits our situation, but this is not an emotional experience either.

It is important to distinguish sensations and thoughts from emotions because of how we deal with them. It is healthy to allow our emotions to "move" and let ourselves fully experience them when that is appropriate to the situation. Emotions are temporary when we allow ourselves to feel them. However, thoughts and sensations are not necessarily temporary. Focusing on a thought or sensation can amplify or expand it. This is especially true of wants and desires. Going with what we want or "feel" about some things may or may not be helpful at all and could lead to disaster. Saying "I feel like the stock market will go up" is probably not a good reason to invest all our money in stocks. In general, whenever we say something that begins with "I feel that..." or "I feel like...," we are talking about thoughts or sensations rather than emotions.

Thoughts get confused with emotions in more subtle ways, too. Examples are guilt and hatred. We often think of these as emotions, but in fact they are primarily mental constructs. We may experience emotions when we think about these concepts, but they need to be distinguished from true emotions because they require a different response. Guilt does involve a feeling or emotion of sadness or hurt about something we have done, but it is more a process of thinking about our offense and regretting it. There is emotion mixed in with guilt, but the primary experience involves thinking about what we did. Allowing ourselves to experience guilt as if it were an emotion tends to feed and expand it.

Similarly, hatred adds thoughts of animosity and revenge to emotions of hurt, frustration, or anger. Clearly, allowing ourselves to "feel" hatred and to let it "move" is not a healthy thing.

Focusing on thoughts and sensations is a very different experience from feeling our emotions. For example, a client who comes in with a lot of emotional tension may say they "feel that" something is unfair or they "feel like" someone is being insensitive to them. This rarely helps them let go of tension but rather seems to build it up. When they finally acknowledge a true emotion, for example, that they "feel hurt and sad," then the tension starts to let go. They usually have a good cry and then we are able to clarify what is unfair or unjust and what they can do about it.

Thoughts Feed Emotions

Chapter Nine described how emotions are a response to our perceptions at the moment. It is very easy for thoughts to dominate our perceptions. Thinking about a loss can make us feel sad. Dwelling on the loss continues our sadness. It is normal to think about intense emotional experiences. But when our thoughts get stuck there, our emotions just keep going. The result is emotional recycling. Chapters Eight and Thirteen described how our mind seems to be drawn to areas of tension in our lives. If we are tensing to prevent experiencing our emotions, it is possible to create a vicious circle where thoughts and emotion each stimulate more intensity in the other. Our thoughts are drawn to our emotions and our emotions stimulate more intense thoughts. This, in turn, stimulates stronger emotions which increase the force of our thoughts. The solution is to relax and to redirect our thoughts. The approaches described in the previous three chapters help us to do this.

"Talking About" and Expressing Our Feelings

Talking about our emotions with a person who is understanding and supportive often helps us to feel better. However, it is important to clarify when this is helpful and when it can lead to the emotional recycling described above. We generally feel better when we sense that we are understood and supported. Part of understanding and supporting another person involves recognizing what they are feeling. Talking about emotions can help us to get in touch with our feelings. This is a healthy experience if we then allow ourselves to experience the emotion and let it go. However, if we tense against the emotion, talking about it without letting it go increases our tension. Talking about emotional events stimulates new emotions and is only helpful to the extent that it helps us clarify what we are feeling and facilitates letting go of emotional tension. Talking about our feelings leads to emotional recycling if we build tension by holding back some of the emotion or if we continue to go over the same events again and again without finding resolution.

Physically expressing emotions is not necessary and, in some cases, not appropriate. Shouting or hitting a punching bag may tire us out, but it rarely relieves specific areas of tension that result from built-up anger. There are very precise exercises that have been designed to release tension in specific areas of the body where it tends to build up in response to holding on to anger or frustration, but these need to be practiced with proper training or supervision and are beyond the scope of this book. What is most important is to identify and experience our emotions. In many cases, this can be done quietly without a lot of noisy expression. Talking about or expressing our emotions is helpful only to the extent that it helps us get in touch with and then let go of our feelings.

Anger: A Unique Emotion

Anger is different from other emotions in two ways. First, it is not a primary emotion. Anger always comes from another emotion. Any time we are angry, there is another emotion that came first. Anger tends to overpower the other emotion because it is so much stronger. Yet, if we take time to look at it, the underlying emotion is always apparent. I may feel angry when someone cuts me off on the highway, but the primary feeling was fear. I may feel angry when someone makes a joke at my expense, but the primary feeling is hurt or embarrassment. I may feel angry about a loss of something important to me, but the primary feeling is sadness.

Second, the function of anger is to push others away from us. This works in the animal kingdom. When an angry dog growls, we back away. Sharing emotions with someone who understands our experience creates a bond or connection. People who have shared a frightening experience or a major loss often feel closer afterwards. Not so with anger. Since anger pushes people away, it tends to damage relationships.

Anger always stimulates the sympathetic nervous system and sends energy to our muscles so that we are ready to attack if needed. The most helpful thing to do when we begin to feel angry is to take slow, even breaths that rhythmically move the diaphragm (Chapter Eleven), shift into a more grounded position (Chapter Twelve), and then step back and clarify the primary emotion. It is much easier to work out a situation where there is frustration, fear, hurt, or embarrassment than it is to deal with anger. Anger needs to be defused. It is not productive unless we are in a life-threatening situation, and even then, only if it serves the purpose of keeping the source of danger away from us. We tend to "lose our head" when we are angry. We give in to impulses without considering the consequences. Anger either builds tension or causes destruction.

Anger and stress tend to feed each other, since both involve the build-up of tension. We are more likely to lose our temper as we become more stressed. We are also more likely to become stressed as we get more angry. Balance is the key, in my experience, to helping people who have problems with anger. Getting into balance reduces the tension that intensifies the anger, and allows enough space for us to accept and clarify what's happening and to see what we can do about it.

Compounded Emotions

Not accepting an emotion can compound its effects. For example, if I begin to feel embarrassed and then start to worry about what others will think if I look embarrassed, I become even more embarrassed. Becoming embarrassed about being embarrassed compounds our embarrassment. This is particularly true with anxiety; it is a common source of panic attacks. We begin to feel anxious and then to worry about the fact that we're anxious. This makes us still more anxious. If we tense up to try to control our anxiety, things get even worse. The same is true with being afraid of being afraid or being frustrated about being frustrated. The problem lies in thinking that we shouldn't be experiencing a particular emotion. If we simply allow ourselves to feel a little embarrassed and let it pass, we soon become interested in what is going on and are no longer embarrassed.

Emotions are natural human responses. We may not like some of them, but they are part of our lives. To the extent that we deny our emotions, we deny life and create tension which keeps us from also experiencing pleasure, joy, and love.

Linked Emotions

Many emotions can be linked to concepts, beliefs, or perceptions that can often be clarified to reveal choices about dealing with recurrent or troublesome feelings. For example, frustration is linked to an expectation. We only become frustrated to the extent that an outcome is unexpected. If we experience a lot of frustration, it can be helpful to evaluate how realistic or helpful our expectations may be.

Feeling confused is usually linked with a lack of information or a perspective that does not fit the information we have. Clarifying available information or exploring other perspectives can lead either to dispelling the confusion or to accepting that further clarification is not available at the time.

Embarrassment commonly involves a certain context as well as a belief about how people are viewing us. Clarifying the context and belief can help us understand the implications of the situation, possibly reduce our embarrassment, and likely help us to learn from the experience.

Feeling afraid is linked to some kind of a threat. Clarifying the nature and severity of the threat, along with its likely consequences can help us either let go of the fear or face it with better preparation.

Discovering links in emotions is a process of, first, accepting and allowing ourselves to feel the emotion, and, second, asking questions about the nature, source, context, beliefs, attitudes, or expectations that are associated with that emotion. It is rather like looking around the emotion to see what may be related to it. In many cases we can change or learn from these relationships.

Chapter Fifteen

Nurturing Spiritual Balance

Stress and Spirituality

It is very easy for our spiritual self to be pushed aside and left behind during times of high stress. Stress speeds us up and spins us around so that we lose track of our place in the world. We tend either to over-emphasize or de-emphasize our own importance under stress - indications of the increasing lack of awareness and inflated self-centeredness that stress produces. God does not attempt to compete with our stressors. He lets us choose our own focus and direction, and experience the consequences of our choices and actions.

Happiness and Fulfillment

Spirituality can be thought of as a process of discovering true happiness and fulfillment. Physical pleasure can never be more than momentary - taking any pleasure to excess ultimately leads to discomfort. Material success doesn't lead to long-term happiness or fulfillment either. Studies of lottery winners and people who have achieved quick financial success indicate that, after a time, they are no happier than before their life-changing event. The high divorce rate among so many people who were sure that they had met the "right" person is clear evidence that romance doesn't necessarily lead to long-term fulfillment. Much of our stress comes from cultural pressure to achieve, accomplish, and obtain things that only bring us temporary satisfaction at best. We continually strive for more because we are heading in a direction that always leads to not enough.

Life satisfaction, happiness, and fulfillment appear to be highly correlated with spiritual beliefs, according to recent polls and surveys. A Gallup poll revealed that people who feel loved by God and who identify spirituality as the most important influence in their lives are twice as likely to report that they are "very happy" as people who don't share those beliefs. A National Opinion Research Center survey found that people who had suffered a major loss were more likely to be happy with their lives to the extent that they had a strong spiritual commitment.

I believe there are a number of components of spirituality that explain the link between being happy and fulfilled and maintaining a regular spiritual practice. The spiritual life promotes harmony, peace of mind, appreciation, acceptance, forgiveness, compassion, and love. Seeking these experiences becomes a way of life rather than a struggle to achieve an objective. Where we are going becomes more important than where we are. Direction matters more than status.

Our spirituality puts us in touch with how we fit in the larger scheme of things. We realize that we are loved, that we have an important role to play, and that this is a process that lasts our entire life.

Spirituality promotes compassion, which helps us realize that we are not alone and that what we have in common with other people is much greater than our differences. We recognize that other points of view are valid, and that none of us has all the answers. Spirituality puts us in touch with what is real and important at each moment in time. Stress diminishes spirituality by turning moments into a blur that blends into the background as we rush around and get stuck in search of something that has been right inside and next to us all along.

Regaining Spiritual Balance

There are no stressed-out saints or spiritual leaders. Regular practice of spiritual discipline undermines stress by keeping us in touch with God, who clearly does not want us to be stressed out. This doesn't mean that we will not experience pain and suffering if we follow a spiritual practice. Quite the contrary. A deepening spiritual practice puts us more in touch with the world, which is partially a place of pain and suffering. The stories of saints and great spiritual leaders are descriptions of people who have been able to transcend pain and suffering to discover a deeper life beyond.

High stress and a deepening spirituality are mutually exclusive. Stress diminishes our awareness, while spirituality puts us more in touch with life. Striving for spiritual growth brings a greater appreciation of the value and opportunities inherent in each moment. Stress builds so much momentum that individual moments turn into frames in an action movie. Stress feeds on regret over the past and worry about the future. Spirituality helps us recognize that everything happens in the present.

Regaining spiritual balance is a process of recognizing priorities, remembering centuries-old lessons, and making choices day by day. It involves a recognition that this life is not heaven but the road to heaven, and that what is most important is not so much where we are on this road but what direction we are headed in.

Establishing and Maintaining a Spiritual Routine

Establishing a daily spiritual routine keeps us moving toward God, or at least facing in that direction. Making room for spirituality on a daily basis keeps us in touch with our values and beliefs. It can take a few weeks to work out and establish a daily spiritual routine. Once in place, it becomes a part of our lives, and we are like "trees planted by streams of water" (Psalm 1:3) receiving regular nourishment for our spiritual needs. It is not necessary to commit to a large block of time when first creating a routine. I started with about five to ten minutes of scripture reading and reflection in the mid-eighties and now set aside the first hour of my day as for spiritual reading and receptive/reflective time.

There are a wide range of books and tapes that can be incorporated into a daily routine. It is important to find something that touches us and fits into our schedule without a lot of ongoing effort. It is easier to establish a routine if we set aside a regular time for practice, such as the first thing in the morning, meal or break time, after dinner, before bed, etc.. Over time we will notice that the increased peace of mind and sense of perspective that this time gives to us is well worth the effort.

Acknowledging, Accepting, Forgiving

Keeping up a regular spiritual routine helps us cultivate attitudes that not only reduce stress but deepen our spiritual awareness. Recognizing that there is a larger reality than our day-to-day existence helps us put our stressors and struggles into a larger perspective. I find it helpful to think of our world as a training camp that teaches us how to love more fully and completely. There was an Olympic swimmer who was reported to have practiced swimming with buckets attached to his legs in order to strengthen his stroke. Athletes take on extra burdens willingly in order to build strength and endurance for their chosen event. Spirituality involves learning to love more deeply and completely. The burdens and struggles we face on this journey provide opportunities to build understanding and endurance in our commitment to become more loving.

Accepting what is presented to us without complaining that it is "not fair" or "should be" somehow different frees us to see the opportunities and gifts in each situation. Refusing to accept events that God allows to take place undermines our trust in God. Acceptance doesn't mean that we say that everything is fine or wonderful - it simply involves acknowledging the reality of our situation without resentment, blame, or "shoulds." (Acceptance is one of three principles of stress management that I will explain in more detail in Section Three.) Refusing to accept a situation or event, in a way, moves us away from love. It closes us to lessons or opportunities that may lie hidden within our struggle or pain.

Practicing forgiveness frees us to see the capacity for love within each person, especially those who have hurt us. Refusing to forgive builds a wall of tension between ourselves and the other person. Anytime there is tension between us and another person, there is tension between us and God. Deciding to forgive takes down spiritual obstacles and reduces physical, mental, and emotional tension as well. Forgiving is essentially a decision to be free from a tension that creates obstacles to love.

Thankfulness

Cultivating an attitude of thankfulness keeps us in touch with the often hidden spirit of love that is part of our daily life. We behave differently when we feel loved

and see manifestations of love each day if we are open to
them. Stress blinds us to beauty and wonder in our world
and leads us to take our gifts for granted. Recognizing and being thankful for all the simple and wonderful
things that bring ease and beauty to our lives helps bring
appreciation and wonder to even difficult times. We
need to slow down to recognize our many gifts. When
we are able to fully appreciate what has been placed in
front us, we can more readily accept the challenges that
have also been given to us.

Compassion

Compassion puts us in touch with the rest of the
world. It is hard to be in conflict with others when we
understand and appreciate their experience. There is no
room for compassion in a stress-filled life. It takes time
to listen and to feel what others experience. This very act
puts us in touch with ourselves and with God as well as
with other people. We don't need to change the world
to be compassionate. Mother Teresa said that we can
only love one person at a time. This means that we take
time for each person we come in contact with and recognize the potential for love within them. It is impossible to maintain a stressed-out lifestyle if we incorporate
compassion for ourselves and others into our lives.

Trust

Stress can be seen as a process that undermines our
trust in God. If we fully trust God and constantly strive
to discern His will, there is no need for tension or struggle. Feeling overwhelmed or under pressure is incon-
sistent with an understanding that we are always loved
and that everything exists for a higher purpose. Thomas
Merton included in his book "Thoughts in Solitude" a

prayer which exemplifies an attitude of trust in God that leaves us open to whatever experiences we encounter:

> *My Lord God, I have no idea where I am going. I do not see the road ahead of me. I cannot know for certain where it will end. Nor do I really know myself, and the fact that I think I am following your will does not mean that I am actually doing so. But I believe that the desire to please you does in fact please you. And I hope I have that desire in all that I am doing. I hope that I will never do anything apart from that desire. And I know that if I do this, you will lead me by the right road though I may know nothing about it. Therefore will I trust you always though I may seem to be lost and in the shadow of death. I will not fear because you are ever with me, and you will never leave me to face my perils alone.*

Humility

Stress makes us more self-centered and self-absorbed. Humility keeps us in touch with reality. Stress and tension compel us to become more preoccupied with our own "stuff" - whether it be our position, belongings, stature, and striving for success or survival, or our pain, hurt, loss, and fear. Humility helps us recognize that we are part of something much larger than ourselves and that we are not alone.

We nourish our spirituality and undermine stress to the extent that we keep in touch with God throughout our daily activities. There are dozens of opportunities each day to give thanks for all of the gifts that make our lives easier. Trusting that there can be meaning and purpose in our pain and struggles frees us from building tension by trying to resist what is already there. Acknowledging and accepting that we are a part of something much larger than we can ever conceive keeps us open to life and its many opportunities. Taking steps to counteract the ways in which stress limits our spirituality keeps us in touch with ourselves, our surroundings, and God.

Part Three

Dealing With It
Day-to-Day

Chapter Sixteen

Principles of Stress Management

Adapt and Improve

I remember learning two ways to build a fire as a Boy Scout. One instructor showed us how to meticulously stack kindling and larger pieces of wood into a carefully constructed pyramid. This method worked when we had the right size and shape of sticks and firewood. But we were lost when the materials at hand didn't match what the instructor had taught us. We also failed during a winter camp-out when we tried to build a fire in a wood stove where the pyramid didn't fit.

Another adult took us aside and said: "Just remember three principles: A fire needs fuel, heat, and air. If you give it what in needs in an amount it can handle, you'll build a good fire every time." It worked. We saw that small pieces of wood burned hotter but that they needed to be spaced far enough apart to allow air to circulate. We also learned that closely spaced wood generated more heat as it reflected off two or more surfaces. It became easy to build a fire, and we got better and better as we were challenged by new situations. I can now build a fire pretty much anywhere, even on a canoe trip after two days of continuous rain had soaked all of the wood.

I have found the same sort of thing to be true with baking. Following a recipe exactly teaches us how to bake one kind of bread. Understanding the principles of the relationship between liquid and flour, and how yeast, sugar, and gluten affect rising, allows us to adapt recipes to our family's tastes and preferences. We can use different kinds of flour to alter the texture. If the loaf doesn't rise enough, the principles of bread baking can help us improve it the next time.

Principles provide direction while allowing us to adapt and improve to fit each unique situation. Applying principles allows us to respond to real-life situations with sensitivity and flexibility. They provide a guide and framework for our thoughts and actions without telling us exactly what to do. Principles get us started in a helpful direction and then give us the freedom to continue learning and improving.

Principles of Stress Management[3]

When I first started teaching stress-management workshops in the late 1970's, I spent a lot of time reflecting on the underlying principles of what worked when stress was managed effectively. I initially came up with seventeen principles that seemed to get things moving in a positive direction when stress levels began to build. Over the next few years, with additional experience and reflection, I was able to refine and combine these principles until I had narrowed them down to three basic concepts: Accept, Balance, and Clarify (the ABC's of Stress Management).

I eventually realized that these three principles formed the basis for almost everything I did in teach-

[3] I am indebted to Dr. Ralph Lewis, Biologist at Michigan State University for helping me see the value of using principles in teaching.

ing or counseling. They helped when counseling kids, adults, or couples. They were easily adapted to classes and workshops in stress, parenting, communication, conflict resolution, time management, empowerment, dealing with chronic pain, and adapting to chronic or terminal illnesses. If there was uncertainty over what to do, or if things seemed to be stuck or getting worse, applying the ABC's would get them moving in a positive direction. The principles didn't necessarily provide an immediate solution, but they always helped to uncover steps that started things moving in the direction of resolution.

I have asked students and participants in many of my classes and workshops to apply the ABC's of Stress Management in their daily lives and then send me a description of the results. Hundreds of reports over decades of teaching have consistently shown that the principles helped bring a greater sense of ease and calm to stressful situations, while providing direction that led to resolution of stress and conflict. There were a number of instances where applying the principles made dramatic changes in someone's life. Students and workshop participants reported that the principles provided a useful tool that gave them a growing confidence that they could effectively manage stress and prevent it from interfering with their lives.

The Principles of Stress Management are not a magic formula that will immediately fix everything that is wrong. They are simply a common-sense set of concepts that help us to deal with our struggles more effectively. The purpose of the principles is to help us reverse the build-up of stress and take positive steps that lead to resolution of our difficulties and a greater sense of ease and satisfaction in our work, health, and relationships.

Applying the ABC's

I call the principles of stress management the ABC's because that makes them as easy to remember as the first three letters of the alphabet. However, I don't apply them in that order. My experience has been that it is always most helpful to begin with the principle of Balance. Starting with the principles of Accepting and Clarifying can help, but regaining physical, mental, emotional, and spiritual balance makes it easier to apply the other two principles. There have been a lot of situations where I have seen an obvious way to apply the principles of Accept or Clarify right away, but I have learned to back up and focus on balance first. Being out of balance complicates everything else by limiting our perceptions and receptivity. Restoring even some degree of balance stops the build-up of pressure and allows us to access more of our resources in confronting a problem. Sometimes being out of balance is the whole problem.

A woman in a parenting workshop brought up a concern about a conflict between her 7-year-old son and his teacher. She went into great detail about the level of misunderstanding between them and the unfairness that she perceived in the situation. She stated that her son had absolutely no problems with last year's teacher but just couldn't get along with his current one. I saw very obvious ways to apply the principles of Accept and Clarify in order to try to create better communication and cooperation with the school, but held back and asked about balance first: "Has anything changed in your family from last year to this year?" The mother said, "Well, yes. Last year I was a stay-at-home mom. This year I'm working full time and also going to school full time. I'm actually taking twenty credits so I can get my degree in less than two years."

Further questioning revealed that her son had a tendency to be quite active, and that the previous year they had gone swimming almost every day after school. Now he went home to a baby sitter and spent his afternoons watching TV. The previous year, the mother had been around all the time and he had lots of opportunity to discharge the build-up of tension from sitting in school all day. Suddenly, he saw little of his mother and had no physical outlets. His mother later reported to me that adjusting her schedule to spend more time with him and making sure he had the opportunity for lots of physical activity had made it easier for him to sit still and concentrate in the classroom. The problems with the teacher disappeared as her son regained more balance in his life, and he became less disruptive in the classroom.

Balance

Everything is easier when we are in balance. Everything is harder when we are out of balance. Balance allows us to slow down enough so that we can see more clearly, listen more intently, and discern more accurately the needs of the situation. Events that can create tidal waves in our lives when we are severely out of balance can have no more effect than ripples on a pond when we make balance a priority. Most of this book thus far has been about balance. Chapters Seven through Ten describe how we get out of balance while Chapters Eleven through Fifteen explain how to get back into balance.

Applying the principle of Balance primarily involves recovering from and preventing the build-up of tension. It also applies to our activities and relationships. We need balance between different kinds and levels of activity, between busy and quiet times, times spent alone or with others, times that are planned or spontaneous.

Stressful times need to be balanced with times that are refreshing and relaxing. We need balance within relationships in terms of control and decision-making and balance within teams and partnerships in terms of work load and leadership.

Balance keeps us even-tempered and level-headed; it helps keep our feet on the ground, our minds clear and our emotions appropriate. It is helpful to pay attention to balance whenever we are confronted with a problem, because we see and think more clearly when we are in balance. We also learn better when in balance. Educational research has shown that we learn the most in the first twenty to thirty minutes of studying. It makes sense to take a break every half-hour if we want to maximize our efficiency. My students regularly report that they get better grades when incorporating balance into their schedule.

Paying attention to other people's balance levels can make a big difference in our relationships. The best time to bring up a concern is when the other person is most receptive and has time to respond appropriately. Bringing up a problem after a long, stressful day or when someone is under pressure or in a hurry is unlikely to lead to resolution. It is more likely to increase the stress levels and further complicate the problem.

The first thing to think about when we begin to recognize the build-up of stress and tension is how to restore balance within ourselves and in the situation. Making balance a priority in our lives leads to a greater sense of ease and calm in day-to-day activities and to more pleasure and satisfaction in our work, health, and relationships.

Accept

Acceptance brings us freedom. It helps us avoid the trap of getting caught up in resentment, blame, or expectations of what "should be." Acceptance means recognizing what is and moving on from there. This frees us to respond to stress and conflict in a healthy way. Not accepting creates distractions that build tension and interfere with problem solving. Refusing to accept the reality of a situation increases our stress and pain while doing nothing to resolve problems and conflicts. Holding on to and recycling old resentments, disappointments, and "shoulds" keeps us stuck in the past and takes away the opportunity for fresh, new ways of seeing things. Accepting things as they are allows us to see opportunities for improving them.

The principle of Acceptance doesn't mean that everything is OK or wonderful. Sometimes things are as bad as they seem. Acceptance is simply a recognition of what is real without getting stuck in thinking about what should or shouldn't have happened. Acceptance keeps us in the present and allows us to look to the future: it enables us to play the cards we were dealt without complaining about wanting a better hand.

Accepting pain seems to diminish that pain. There is a tendency to tense up when we are in pain and tension magnifies and intensifies pain. Allowing ourselves to feel what is there makes pain much more manageable. Chapters Nine and Fourteen describe how accepting emotions allows them to pass. Not accepting our emotions makes us hold onto them, which creates tension and leads to depression and anxiety.

When our stress involves relationships with others, acceptance means recognizing the essential dignity and worth of each person and being able to separate that essence from the behavior that was involved in our stress. Acceptance involves putting ourselves in another's shoes and understanding their feelings and perspective. When people do not feel accepted they become defensive, which puts up a wall that becomes a major obstacle to resolving conflicts. It is very difficult to have a positive, long-term influence on another person if they do not feel accepted by us.

Acceptance doesn't mean that we approve of everything that someone else does; it involves separating a person from their actions or their situation. Accepting another person opens the door to communication and resolution. Not doing so closes that door.

Acceptance builds tolerance, patience, and empathy. It leads to a clearer understanding of any problem and gives us the flexibility to respond according to the needs of the situation.

Clarify

Stress narrows our focus and limits our perceptions and understanding. Clarifying involves seeing "what is true" from varying perspectives. When we clarify our words, feelings, and impressions, we communicate so that others can understand and respond appropriately. When we clarify values and priorities, we make decisions that lead to success. When we clarify problems and concerns, we gain insight that leads to solutions. Clarifying involves looking at situations from various perspectives and asking questions that help us see the whole picture and relevant details more clearly.

Stress and tension lead to confusion, misunderstanding, and mishandling of people and situations. Pressure and hurry can turn important details, as well as the larger picture, into a blur that can't very well enter into our awareness or decision-making. Clarifying involves stopping what we are doing and taking a good look at what is happening. It usually involves asking questions, breaking things down into workable components, or looking at the big picture.

When stress and tension are building, every problem and concern appears to demand our immediate attention. Restoring balance and then separating concerns into immediate, short-term, and long-term issues allows us to efficiently focus on one thing at a time and develop and adapt strategies that lead to effective solutions that last. Clarifying our values and priorities provides direction for our efforts. Clarifying options, obstacles, and opportunities helps us discern what is possible. Clarifying expectations, assumptions, and beliefs allows us see what is realistic and what may be unproductive. Clarifying strengths makes it possible for us to use all of the resources available. Clarifying weaknesses and limitations helps us identify what we need and how others may be helpful. Clarifying helps us know how things work, where we stand, what we face, where we're headed, and what is likely or at least possible.

Clarifying a situation often makes it easier to accept it. Likewise, accepting a situation makes it easier to clarify. Both are easier to the extent that we are in balance. The ABC's of Stress Management work together, with each reinforcing the other. It is helpful to start with balance and then to work on accepting, clarifying, or balancing some more as the needs of the situation indicate. Learning to apply these principles to life's situations is a skill that develops and improves with practice.

Chapter Seventeen

Applying the ABC's to Common Stressors

Same Principles, Different Situations

I often ask clients, students, and workshop participants to identify the major sources of stress in their lives.
The most common responses include work, school, parenting, relationships, health, and too much to do. This
chapter outlines some considerations for applying the
ABC's of Stress Management to each of these concerns.
The purpose is not to provide a comprehensive plan of
how to address these stressors but simply to provide
some examples of how the principles might be applied
in various situations. The principles are listed separately
in order to illustrate how each principle might be applied
in a particular kind of situation. In dealing with specific
instances, it is likely that we will use the principles in-
terchangeably rather than in any particular order (except
that it is always best to start with Balance).

Work and Organizational Stress

Work stress usually involves problems in relationships with employees, co-workers, or supervisors; or issues related to work load or working conditions.

Balance

Organizational stress is more likely to build up from day-to-day hassles and frustrations rather than from single catastrophic events. These stressors tend to persist over time, and it is not unusual for us to spend a large portion of our day in a stressful environment. For these reasons, it can be very helpful to identify opportunities and to establish a routine for maintaining balance and preventing the build-up of tension.

Pressure and hurry build tension which interferes with efficiency and effectiveness. We can maintain balance under a heavy work load by searching for opportunities throughout the day to practice grounding, Thought Refocusing and/or Natural Rhythmic Breathing. Simply taking a single rhythmic diaphragmatic breath before answering the phone, for example, can break the build-up of tension and help us shift gears for a new demand. Linking balancing techniques to regular parts of our daily schedule, such as breaks, transitions before starting new tasks, waiting for computers, etc., helps us to recover from recent stressors and to maintain a clearer perspective.

If our work situation places heavy demands on us, it becomes even more important to build balance into the rest of our lives. Fitting in regular meditation or finding activities that counter work stress helps us to find some balance at the end of each day, rather than getting caught in a continuing spiral of increasing stress.

It is also helpful to consider balance when scheduling and setting priorities for our work. Our energy level and ability to focus on various tasks varies with the kind of work we do and often changes through the day. Identifying what we can realistically accomplish, as well as our own rhythms of work, helps us to schedule activities that match our capacity and keep us fresh and productive.

It is important to consider balance when confronting problems or conflicts at work. An employee, co-worker, or supervisor will be much more receptive to our input if we approach them when both of us are more likely to be in balance. It is helpful to balance constructive criticism with positive feedback, both within a single conversation and over time. We are much more likely to listen to criticism from someone who lets us know on a regular basis that they recognize and appreciate our effort and contribution.

The workplace becomes more balanced when all staff have access to information and a clear sense of the larger picture. Clear, respectful, and open communication builds balance and provides a vehicle for managing and preventing misunderstanding and conflict. Morale and productivity improve when there is balance between control and responsibility. Having too much control when others with too little control are responsible for the work being done easily leads to frustration and inefficiency.

Work becomes more productive and pleasurable when there are opportunities for physical and mental activities that relieve tension and restore balance. Such opportunities result from good communication, access to information, and balance between control and responsibility.

Accept

One of the major stressors in organizations comes from expectations about what "should" be. It is easy to build up resentment by recycling frustrations in our own minds and complaining to co-workers. This significantly adds to the stress response. There are few, if any, perfect organizations. Acknowledging the present limitations of our organization without getting attached to what "should" be reduces stress and frees us to make clear decisions about what is best for us and the organization. Avoiding work-site gossip and "gripe sessions" makes it easier to accept the limitations of our job and to make clear decisions either to resign ourselves to or confront problem areas. Letting go of blame, resentment, and complaining frees us so that we can take a fresh look at the situation and see possible solutions.

When people feel threatened, they become defensive. When we are defensive, it is easy to become closed to input and suggestions. Trying to look at things from the other person's perspective helps broaden our perceptions, and can provide insight into what may be guiding their behavior. Working to understand employees', co-workers', and supervisors' pressures and responsibilities, while recognizing everyone's need for basic respect and forgiveness, helps reduce tension and helps us find solutions that benefit everyone.

Acceptance does not imply that we give up or never try to bring about positive change. Practicing and communicating acceptance allows us to assess the opportunities and timing for lasting change, and builds relationships that make it more likely that improvements will happen.

Clarify

Clarifying involves discerning values and priorities, looking at situations from a variety of perspectives, asking questions, and looking for options that lead to a more complete understanding of what is true and possible. Many job stressors involve the perception of a threat or frustration at some level. Clarifying what might actually be threatening helps us see and deal with the stressor more clearly. Frustration is directly related to expectation. Clarifying our expectations and the limitations of the current situation can keep daily hassles from building into major stressors.

Clarifying how important our job is to us as well as what other opportunities are available helps us find acceptance or make decisions that can reduce work stress. Stressors in a part-time, temporary job are dealt with much differently than in a job that we expect to keep for a number of years. Understanding similarities and differences between our own values and priorities and those of the organization helps us see opportunities and limitations for change and provides support for decision-making.

Clarifying stressors and stress levels of employees, co-workers, and supervisors helps us understand what they might be going through. Asking ourselves questions about the other person's likely receptivity to change, and about how and when this current problem can likely be worked out can guide us in developing a plan to resolve our differences. Clarifying our emotions and the words we use to describe the situation leads us to figuring out how best to approach the other person.

School Stress

School stress usually involves feeling pressure to do well or to get things done, or a sense of being overwhelmed by having too much to do with too little time to complete it.

Balance

Building balance into a school schedule can make a tremendous difference in how we live that schedule day-to-day. Insuring that there is room for breaks between classes and during study times allows us to get things done and to learn more efficiently. If we have underestimated our work load and begin to become overwhelmed, we can actually accomplish more by increasing the time we spend in balancing activities such as Natural Rhythmic Breathing, grounding, and meditation.

Worrying about tests or assignments can waste a lot of time and energy. Using Thought Refocusing with Natural Rhythmic Breathing helps us let go of these worries and focus on the task at hand. Students who meditate regularly report that their sense of ease and relaxation about taking tests or completing assignments improves along with their grades.

Accept

Accepting our limitations and work load can save a lot of energy and tension by helping us to readjust our priorities and expectations. Acknowledging mistakes and failure without blaming ourselves or others frees us to reassess what can be done to improve the situation. Acceptance frees us to do our best work and allows us to maintain focus and concentration.

Clarify

Clarifying goals and priorities can prevent a lot of unnecessary stress. Setting academic goals that match our career goals lets us see what level of performance we need to strive for in our classes. Someone earning a technical degree will benefit most from placing a priority on work that builds skills and has a practical application. Someone who wants to go on to earn an advanced degree in a competitive graduate-school program will need to pay closer attention to grades and to establishing relationships with instructors who may write letters of recommendation.

Clarifying how much time will likely be needed to complete assignments helps us plan ahead and avoid the crunch where everything is due and there is no time left. Spending time reflecting about how we learn best or under what conditions we seem to study best helps us to increase our efficiency and performance.

Parenting

Stressors from parenting tend to be related to frustration about getting children to do what we want them to do, especially when there is pressure or a reason to hurry. Struggling to deal with problems that our children may be having is another major stressor often reported by parents.

Balance

Most problems with children's behavior occur when they are hungry, tired, or frustrated. Paying attention to when our children are out of balance in these areas can prevent a lot of stress and conflict. Many other problems with children's behavior occur when adults are hungry, tired, stressed out, or frustrated. Paying attention to our own balance levels when parenting can prevent even more stress and conflict.

Taking a few natural rhythmic breaths, doing some grounding, and taking some time to apply the principles of Acceptance and Clarifying before intervening with a child can make all the difference in the world. Pressure is often a component of parent-child conflicts; we want something done or something to stop NOW. Recognizing that there is a transition from where we are to where we want things to be helps to relieve that pressure, and increases the likelihood that we will actually accomplish what we intend.

When teaching parenting workshops, I often ask parents to identify characteristics that they want their children to have when they become adults. I suggest that this is the place to focus when dealing with day-to-day hassles. Approaching parenting as a long-term teaching and learning process rather than as a series of short-term roles as a referee or policeman builds patience and perseverance, both of which bring balance to family life.

Conflicts and discipline problems are much easier to resolve when there is an ongoing effort to maintain balance in communication - an equal effort toward listening and informing. Regular family meetings where everyone can discuss concerns and problems can have a substantial impact toward maintaining balance within a family. Balance is also important in choosing consequences; the effects are more likely to "sink in" when there is a clear relationship between the nature and severity of the problem and the consequence.

Accept

Children are more likely to cooperate when they feel accepted and more likely to rebel when they do not feel accepted. There is a huge difference between dealing with problem behavior and dealing with a "problem child." Resolution becomes extremely difficult when a child is seen as the problem. Children do not comprehend how they can change their self. However, they can easily understand how to change their behavior, especially if we provide clear incentives and consequences.

Being able to put ourselves in our children's shoes and see a situation as they see it makes a tremendous difference in our ability to teach them and in their ability to listen to us. Stopping to think "What is she feeling right now?" and communicating that thought to a child is often the difference between a quick resolution and an escalating conflict.

Trying to teach a child something when we are both upset rarely has a positive impact; it is more likely to result in yelling or physical discipline, both of which tend to make children feel afraid and resentful. Fear works over the short term to motivate behavior, but at the cost of trust and respect in the long-term relationship. Accepting that the learning process does not always run smoothly in a straight line helps us be more patient and learn from mistakes.

Clarify

Clarifying in our own mind that every problem and conflict with our children is an opportunity for them to learn an important life lesson helps us put things in perspective and find ways that lead to lasting solutions. Viewing concerns in this way makes us less reactive and helps our children develop skills and capabilities that prevent stress and difficulty. Maintaining focus on the long term makes the job of parenting easier over both the short and long term.

Clarifying what a child is feeling and what they might be trying to accomplish through their behavior gives us valuable insights about how to approach the situation most effectively. Being very clear in the language we use when talking with our children prevents misunderstanding and a lot of potential stress. It is also very helpful to clarify that what they understood is what we intended to say to them. Clarifying what our child is able to understand and do helps keep our expectations more realistic and us more patient.

Teaching and communicating clearly with children of any age requires us to be consistent. That means following through with every promised discipline. It helps to clarify that it is realistic and possible for us to follow through before setting a potential consequence. Saying we will cancel the family vacation if a child's room is not clean is inviting them to test our will power. Giving in after repeated begging and pleading teaches that begging and pleading work. A clear decision to always be consistent saves a lot of time and prevents a lot of stress and hassle.

Primary Relationships

Any relationship that grows must be able to weather stress and conflict. Our partner is the person who knows us best. As two people open up to each other and share more of themselves, there are bound to be overlapping rough spots. Stress in relationships is often related to difficulties in commitment, trust, communication, and/ or problem solving.

Balance

Nothing is more unbalancing for a relationship than to have an uncertain commitment. Marriage vows are the centerpiece of a wedding and a marriage. Having a clear commitment to work things out no matter what (unless there are safety issues) creates a foundation of trust and patience upon which a relationship can grow. Anything we build up or work out without that foundation can quickly crumble. Reaffirming the commitment in a relationship on a regular basis and especially during difficult times maintains the energy and focus necessary to work through inevitable hard times.

When conflicts do arise, taking a few natural rhythmic breaths and doing some grounding can make a huge difference. It is also helpful to check out how our partner is doing in terms of balance and to choose times and places for discussion of difficult issues accordingly.

Relationships that maintain a balance of control and decision-making between partners will tend to have less stress than those that do not. Likewise, striving for balance in work load and responsibility builds a partnership that helps relieve stress rather than build it. Making sure there is time for fun and relaxation as well as work and responsibility adds to balance in a relationship. Also, finding time to be alone and as a couple can prevent stress and tension from building.

Relationships that maintain regular open communication are likely to have less stress than those that do not. Setting aside the time and space to share experiences, ideas, and concerns helps keep a relationship in balance and prevents misunderstanding and a lot of potential tension.

Accept

Accepting the limitations and mistakes of a partner can prevent a lot of stress and conflict. Accepting that conflict will arise in any relationship that is becoming closer allows us to focus on building solutions that strengthen trust and cooperation. Acceptance helps us avoid blame and resentment, which can act like a cancer in a relationship. Acceptance keeps us focused on what we can do to deal with a situation and improve a relationship. Blame and resentment keep us focused on how frustrated and miserable we are, which only leads to more frustration and misery.

"Should" is a nasty word in relationships. Thinking about how our partner "should" be or what they "should" do keeps us from taking responsibility for our own behavior, distracts us from figuring out how to resolve our difficulties, and builds resentment and blame. It can be very helpful for couples to explore realistic ways each of them can make improvements. But thinking in terms of "should" criticizes our partners for not already accomplishing the goals we have set for them. Accepting limitations and shortcomings allows us to see where we are, where we want to go, and how we can get there.

Relationships can only grow when both partners feel accepted by the other. We put up a wall when we do not feel accepted, and that wall cuts off communication and trust. It is very important for people in close relationships to be able to see things from the other's perspective and accept that as a valid way of looking at things. Much of the arguing and adversarial struggles within a relationship can be prevented when acceptance is cultivated and nurtured.

Conflicts are much easier to resolve when there is an atmosphere of acceptance. Getting into balance and establishing mutual acceptance are most often the first steps in resolving difficulties. Cultivating acceptance in a relationship is like planting a seed in good soil where it can grow into a healthy, productive plant. Disregarding the principle of acceptance in a relationship is like trying to plant a seed in hard-pan clay - it takes a whole lot more work to even get a limited harvest.

Clarify

A very common problem that tends to occur in the first years of a relationship results from a misunderstanding of the concept of love. A lot of people believe that love involves feelings of attraction and affection that are like a fuel that keeps a relationship going. When the fuel runs out, the relationship ends. A related misconception is that there is a "right" person for each of us, and that if attraction and affection fade, we must not have chosen the "right" person. Clarifying what love is and what it involves makes it possible to deal with the day-to-day reality of strengthening a relationship.

Putting together a long-term relationship is not like finding two pieces of a jigsaw puzzle that make a perfect fit. It is more like building something out of wood, where each of the pieces needs to be trimmed, planed, and sanded before they can be glued together. Love is the glue that holds a relationship together, but it involves much more than attraction and affection. Simply stated, love is decision. It is a decision to hang in there and work it out through good times and bad, even when there is no attraction or affection. One could make a good case for saying that love really begins when attraction and affection start to fade. It is easy to stay with someone when we feel close to them. Love grows and deepens as we work through the struggles that pull us apart. Being clear about our decision to love avoids a lot of traps that easily undermine a long-term relationship.

Clarifying conflicts helps us discover ways to resolve them. Identifying and understanding feelings, needs, and intentions, and being clear about values and priorities, prevents misunderstanding and makes it possible to find solutions where both partners win. Separating issues and working on them one at a time helps us maintain our focus and balance. Clarifying options and how we can realistically achieve our goals helps us work together to build lasting solutions while creating a stronger partnership. Clarifying obstacles and opportunities for intimacy helps us grow closer. Clarifying issues and situations that divide us allows us to confront and resolve these obstacles.

Asking questions about our relationships makes it possible to discover hidden conflicts and resolve them. Clarifying our schedules and responsibilities makes it possible to work together to accomplish what is most important. Clarifying expectations helps us to sort out what is realistic from what will likely lead to frustration. Clarifying helps us see what's important, what needs to be done, and what we need to let go of.

Health

Stressors related to health include dealing with complications and limitations that result from disability and coping with pain and discomfort.

Balance

Balance is important both to maintain health and to recover from illness or injury. Stress suppresses our immune system, which is the part of our body that fights off and helps us recover from disease and illness. Stimulating the parasympathetic nervous system through Natural Rhythmic Breathing allows our body to heal and helps keep us from getting sick. We feel better and have more energy when there is a balance between rest and activity and when we follow a balanced diet.

It is common to tense our muscles when we experience severe pain. However, tension intensifies the pain and can often lead to other problems. Focusing on our pain can also magnify it. Using Natural Rhythmic Breathing and Thought Refocusing helps us accept the level of pain we are experiencing without increasing it.

Accept

It is easy to get frustrated when we are sick or injured, and to question "Why is this happening to me?" This creates additional tension, which makes us feel more miserable and can contribute to more health problems. Accepting our afflictions allows us to put them into perspective and to make clear choices that can lead to improved health. Accepting our limitations when we are sick or injured gives our body the chance to heal and recover. Accepting the need for rest and letting go of things we "should" be doing allows us to put our energy and focus into recovery, instead of adding stress to an already uncomfortable situation.

Clarify

Obtaining information about our illness or injury can greatly facilitate the coping and healing process. Understanding what is happening to us and what our options are helps us deal with our situation more realistically and make intelligent choices. Clarifying our abilities and limitations allows us to accomplish what we can without further compromising our condition. Clarifying and prioritizing our needs enables us to make sure that the most important things are being taken care of. Finding words and images that accurately describe what we are experiencing and keeping track of the course of our symptoms gives medical providers information that helps them arrive at correct diagnoses and treatment options.

Too Much to Do

Having too much to do keeps us on edge and in a state of tension. It can lead to feelings of being overwhelmed and out of control. Applying the ABC's helps to bring a sense of ease to our activities while increasing our efficiency and effectiveness.

Balance

Balance becomes even more important when we are overloaded. We create extra tension when we push ourselves beyond our usual limits, and it is important to allow time to recover from this build-up of tension. Increasing the time spent practicing Natural Rhythmic Breathing, meditation, and Thought Refocusing allows us to work more efficiently and actually tends to save time over the long run. Working at a steady pace and taking regular breaks helps us maintain focus and concentration. Giving in to the temptation to rush and hurry creates tension, scatters our focus, and leads to mistakes and missed opportunities.

If we do take on more than we can handle in a healthy way, it is very important to build in time for recovery after the stressful time has passed. It can take more than two weeks to fully recover from a brief period of high stress. Failing to find opportunities to create balance in our lives can lead to a high-stress lifestyle which diminishes both our effectiveness and our life satisfaction.

Accept

Accepting our obligations and what we can realistically accomplish enables us to make clear decisions about what is important. Getting trapped into thinking in terms of everything we "should" be doing increases pressure and diminishes our ability to discern what is realistic and practical. Accepting what we cannot accomplish frees us to focus on what we can accomplish.

Clarify

Clarifying values and priorities provides a guide for making clear decisions about what we choose to take on and what we can let go of. Taking time to sort out what is most important to us and how we want to live our lives puts our current situation into a larger perspective and gives us a sense of control and continuity. Replacing the concept of "should" with the phrase "if...then" helps us see likely scenarios and consequences and make decisions that fit our values and priorities.

Chapter Eighteen

Applying the ABC's in Real Life

The following brief accounts are summaries of reports by people who have applied the ABC's to stressful situations in their own lives. Many of the details in the descriptions have been changed in order to protect the privacy of those who shared them with me. However, the ways in which the principles were applied in each situation are real. In most cases, these descriptions are of the person's first attempts at applying the principles.

A Frantic Time

"I received a call that my surgery had been scheduled for the following Wednesday. This gave me less than five days to get everything done, including our flight reservations. Everything was very important to me and was a 'must do.' I expected total cooperation from my husband when I gave him a list of things I wanted him to do. His response was: 'Don't worry about it, these things can wait until we get back.' My first response was anger. He was not respecting my wishes. I was going to have surgery and didn't know how long it would take to recover, and he didn't seem to care. I was in a total panic. I was frustrated and he was not helping.

"I did some Natural Rhythmic Breathing and grounding, and decided to go for a walk (Balance). I thought about my anger and realized I was scared. I'd never had surgery before, and this was serious. We would be in a strange city with no one else around (Clarify). I realized that my husband was trying to help me by taking the pressure off (Accept) and that I wanted to get all this stuff done as a way of feeling in control.

"I went back in the house and apologized to my husband for yelling. I told him I was scared about the surgery. He was very understanding and said he would try to help me. I made a list of things that I felt were most important and asked him which items he would be comfortable with (Clarify). I accepted that what got done, got done, and what didn't could wait (Accept).

"I feel like I actually accomplished more by being relaxed, and I learned that I tend to burden myself with unnecessary demands."

Eight-Year-Old Cleaning Her Room

"I sent Rebecca to clean her room while I worked on the rest of the house. About two hours later, I checked on her and she hadn't even started. I was about to blow my top. I walked away and took several deep breaths and did some bouncing (grounding) (Balance). I went back into her room and we talked about what was making it hard for her to clean her room (Accept and Clarify). The room was such a mess, she didn't know where to begin. I suggested we break up the room into parts and that she clean one part at a time (Clarify). I brought up the timer and we set up a goal for how long it would take to do the first section. It turned into a game of beat the clock. I gave her a treat after she finished the first section, and we agreed that she would take a break after finishing each section."

The Obnoxious Dog

"Some friends asked me to house sit and take care of their animals while they were on vacation. They had already left by the time I got there. From the moment I walked in, their dog was absolutely obnoxious. He jumped on me, scratched my legs, and would not obey my commands to sit or stay. I was quite angry. Then I decided to use the ABC's. I locked the dog in the bedroom. Then I took some deep, even breaths to calm myself. I bent my knees and bounced a few times to ground myself (Balance). I accepted the fact that this was the way the dog was acting and let go of my feeling that the dog 'should' obey me (Accept). Then I tried to clarify. I was angry. What other emotion was causing my anger? I realized I was feeling frustration and a loss of control. I was frustrated because I expected the dog to do what I said (apparently my friends hadn't told the dog that). (Clarify). I started to think about how I could get this dog to be tolerable until my friends got home (Accept and Clarify). Then it came to me. The dog had been cooped up all day. My friends had left that morning, and I came after work (Clarify). I took the dog out for a walk and he was a lot calmer after that (Balance). So was I."

Argument With a Friend

"I got into an argument with my boyfriend about why he wasn't returning my phone calls. He accused me of not returning his calls (which wasn't true). At first I was angry, and then I balanced myself mentally and physically by practicing Natural Rhythmic Breathing and Thought Refocusing. I tried to accept what he was saying and clarify what he really meant (he doesn't usually lie to me). We talked some more after we were both in better balance. We figured out that we were both feeling unimportant to the other (Accept and Clarify). He wasn't returning my calls because he thought I was calling purposely when he was at work so I could say I called without having to talk to him. I realized I never paid much attention to what his work schedule was (Clarify). We talked it out calmly and both felt better and more secure."

Hosting a Sleep-Over

"On Friday night I decided to host a sleep-over with my niece (9 years old) and her two friends. What was I thinking? After we ate pizza and I cleaned up, the girls started to get bored. They were arguing with each other, begging, and hanging on me, and I felt I was going to explode. I tried to suggest activities, and I tried to talk to them, but they wouldn't listen. They were either getting into something they couldn't play with, arguing with one another, or begging for my attention. I could feel the tension slowly fill my back and make its way up my neck.

"To make it through the night, I knew I needed to deal with this tension before it got worse. I convinced the girls to paint each other's fingernails while I went into the bathroom. While in the bathroom, I did some Natural Rhythmic Breathing and some grounding exercises (Balance). I realized I had been on the go all day and had had no time to relax, even for a few minutes (Accept and Clarify). I took this time to just sit and clear my thoughts. I read a magazine and let myself completely relax (Balance). I began to think about how I was going to entertain my niece and her friends for the rest of the night (Clarify). I accepted the fact that they were young and excited and that they considered me someone they could have fun with. I also reflected on the idea that when I was nine, I too had bountiful energy and a short attention span (Accept). I started to think of ways to make all of us happy for the rest of the night. A game, a movie, or girl talk - I came to the conclusion that I could make this work (Clarify). A while later, I returned to the girls. I felt relaxed and certain that I would be able to control the situation.

"I know that if I hadn't taken the time to balance myself and to think about what I was going through, I could have really had a negative attitude toward my niece and her friends. I could have made the situation miserable for everyone. By making sure I was clear and secure in the way I was feeling, I was able to listen to them, tolerate them, and even enjoy myself."

Construction in the Kitchen

"Currently I am living with my parents and they are redoing their kitchen floor. The house is a mess, filled with dust and workers. Everything that was in our kitchen is now either in the dining room or the living room. I am beginning to feel angry and frustrated (Clarify). I came home from work today and had no stove, no front door (which caused the house temperature to drop dramatically), and no place to go. I started to feel the stress build up and all I wanted to do was cry or scream. Not to mention that this situation has made me unbearable to live with, and, that there is tension between my parents and me as well as between my parents and the men they have hired to have the floor done before Thanksgiving (which is not looking good).

"When I realized I was getting too stressed to function, I went into the basement. I stretched, I practiced Natural Rhythmic Breathing, and I regained my balance. After doing so I decided to meditate for a while (Balance). After completing my meditation

I started to assess the situation (Clarify). I accepted the fact that my parents had good intentions in re-decorating and that they too were feeling stressed out (Accept). I also came to realize that this situation is not going to last forever and that when it is all done I will be thankful. This clarified what I was going through and allowed me to accept the situation. I was allowed to be disappointed with the fact that things weren't going as planned, but my clarifying and accepting the situation, meant that this did not have to result in more tension for me or my family (Accept and Clarify).

"That evening, I noticed that my mom was getting very stressed out. She was upset, her body ached, and she was full of tension (Accept and Clarify). I had her try Natural Rhythmic Breathing, and I helped her balance herself and work some of the tension out of her body (Balance). She felt better. I felt better, and I can guarantee that the rest of my family felt better. The situation with my house is still the same, but I am able to understand what is going on and therefore can prevent the tension."

Lost Study Time

"Today was my day to study. It started out slow and ended up crazy. I never got a chance to study. I was angry and upset. I felt like a failure. First I balanced myself by doing the Natural Rhythmic Breathing for about fifteen minutes (Balance). Then I accepted that I had not been able to study and realized that I still had time before the tests. I clarified that all the unplanned events that came up were more important than studying (Accept and Clarify). I felt a load lifted from my shoulders when I realized that. I knew there would be another day for studying."

Late Co-Worker

"Today I was supposed to get out of work at noon. The person who was supposed to relieve me wasn't there by 1 p.m.. I was so mad. I had a lot of stuff I wanted to do. The later she was, the more angry I became. I don't like being so upset, so I decided to ground (Balance). After centering myself, I accepted that I wouldn't get to do everything that I wanted to do that day. I realized that it was no big deal, and that I could make it up the next day (Accept and Clarify). When my co-worker finally came in, she apologized for being late. I was calm, but told her I would appreciate her calling if she was going to be late because I had stuff to do (Clarify). She apologized again and told me she had been up late having a big argument with her boyfriend and then had overslept. I felt better after understanding her reasons and was glad that I hadn't yelled at her."

Interruptions and Unexpected Events

"My secretary went home sick today and there were a million things I needed to get done before my boss left on a trip. When Carol is not available, it means that I answer the phones, and this is my biggest distraction. My office is open and people are wandering in and out all of the time. I have constant interruptions, and to add the phones to the intense energy level drives me nuts. After about 8 phone calls, I decided I needed to get a grip on what was happening because I realized that I was becoming very short-tempered with the people who were calling and that it was inappropriate and unprofessional (Accept). I remembered what we talked about in class and started practicing the Natural Rhythmic Breathing (Balance). I took a breath before answering each call, and made sure I had closure on one thing before moving on to the next one (Clarify and Balance).   I decided to put the phones on voice mail every 30 minutes or so.   I would leave the phone on voice mail for about 15 minutes so I could catch my breath and return the calls I had (Clarify and Balance). Then I decided to put the voice mail on whenever I had someone stop in my office who needed my attention to work out a problem (Accept and Balance). Again, what a life-saver, because most of the people who stop in my office need only a few minutes of my time if we aren't interrupted.

"I feel much more relaxed and in control of my day now that I have this system worked out when my secretary is not available to answer the phones. I learned that I am able to think more clearly and am more efficient when I stay in balance and do one thing at a time. I had clearer priorities and accomplished a lot more."

Terminal Illness

"I have a terminal illness for which there is no cure. I've been tense and angry and upset. I started to practice Natural Rhythmic Breathing and then started to pray. I didn't pray to get well. I prayed for peace of mind - for my thoughts to stop racing and the tension to go away (Balance). This didn't happen all at once, but I realized that there was nothing I could do about the fact that I was going to die. There was something I could do about how I was going to live the rest of my life (Accept and Clarify). Once I accepted that I was going to die, I felt like a weight was lifted off my shoulders. I've set some priorities. People I want to spend time with, things that I want to get done before I am too sick to do them (Clarify). Some days I am able to accomplish some things; other days I'm just too tired. When I'm too tired I just rest and breath, and pray, and don't think about what I'm not getting done (Accept and Balance). The other day I started choking. I couldn't catch my breath. I was really tensing up. For a moment, I thought it was the end. I remembered what I learned and tried to relax and take a really slow breath. After a few moments it worked. I was OK (Balance)."

Long Line, in a Hurry

"Waiting in long lines drives me bananas. This time it was at McDonald's. The line was long, moving slowly. Lots of parents with children who had no idea about what they wanted to eat; clerks who appeared to be new on the job.

"Get in balance! I actually got rapidly grounded by 'bouncing' in the line. I don't think anyone realized what I was doing. There was music coming over the speakers, so I just bounced to the beat. It was actually fun, and I forgot about the long wait (Balance). Once I was grounded, I accepted the situation. The weather was bad. It would take longer to drive somewhere else for lunch, and they would probably be busy too (Accept and Clarify). I decided to wait it out and make the best of the situation. I could see what the stress was doing to the others waiting in line, and I decided to stay clear of that. I would eventually get my lunch and I might as well enjoy it rather than be so upset that I couldn't eat (Accept and Clarify).

"I did not get stressed. I got my lunch and had fun 'bouncing' while waiting in line. The clerks seemed to appreciate a friendly customer. Smiles and a friendly, positive attitude to things goes a long way."

Getting a Four-Year-Old Out the Door

"We were running late. My wife had just yelled at our four-year-old son for the third time to put his shoes and coat on. He was in his room looking at a book. I took a few rhythmic breaths and decided to try the ABC's (Balance). I went in my son's room and said: 'Wow, that looks like a neat book' (Accept). He started to tell me about it. I said: 'We're going to be really late if we don't leave now, how 'bout if you show it to me in the car' (Clarify). He put his coat and boots on and less than a minute later was in the car."

Chronic Pain

"My back pain was at about a seven on a ten-point scale on the first day of the workshop. After practicing the Natural Rhythmic Breathing and grounding for two weeks, I got it down to around a four (Balance). I also found out that accepting what I can't do helps me figure out what I can do. I know that I will have some pain all my life, and instead of getting frustrated and impatient and then hurting myself, I'm starting to learn what my limits are (Accept and Clarify). When I feel my back start to tense up, I rest and take note of what I was doing. I always thought I had to finish whatever I started. Now I realize that taking a break when it starts to hurt keeps it from hurting a lot more (Accept, Clarify and Balance). There are some things I will always need help with, but I'm learning that I can do more than I thought, with less pain."

Acute Pain

"I had a good opportunity to practice the relaxation techniques this week. I was driving home when I started to feel some pain in my back. It seemed to get worse after I got home, and then I started to feel sick. I had a lot to do, but this just didn't feel right. Instead of pushing myself and keeping my appointments, I cleared my schedule to take care of myself (Accept and Balance). It was a good thing, too. Shortly after I hung up the phone, I started to get really bad pains in the corner of my back. I lay on the bed and almost started to cry. I could feel myself tensing as the pain got worse. I remembered about tension intensifying pain and started to do the Natural Rhythmic Breathing. It was really hard to focus on it because I was also getting scared. I had no idea what was going on. My mind was racing. I started repeating a short prayer with my breathing. I had to start over and over again, but after awhile I was able to keep it going and the pain eased up a bit. I started thinking about what part of my body was causing the pain. I realized that it was coming from the area around my kidneys. I called a friend and asked her to take me to the emergency room (Clarify). The pain was still pretty intense, but it wasn't as bad as long as I continued breathing and repeating my prayer (Balance). The doctor told me I had a kidney stone. He gave me some medicine to help with the pain, and I used that along with the breathing and my prayer until the stone passed a few days later."

Teen-Age Responsibility

"My sons are fifteen and seventeen. They are not very good at following through with responsibilities, and I always wind up picking up after them and finishing things they were supposed to do. When they asked if they could have a swimming party, I decided it was a good time to practice the ABC's. I told them I would think about it and we could talk after dinner. I did some Natural Rhythmic Breathing and grounding as I planned my strategy (Balance). I did not want to do all the work to clean up the place, get the pool ready, and make food for a party that I would have to clean up after. I told them I would make the food but the rest was up to them. They agreed, and everything looked fine (Clarify). I'd like to be able to say they did all the work without any problem, but that's not the way it happened. They had other things to do, and the day of the party came, and the house was a mess, and the pool hadn't been cleaned. I was frantic. How could they be so irresponsible? Then I remembered to do my breathing and grounding and changed my 'should' thinking to 'if ... then' (Balance, Accept and Clarify). If they wanted to have all their friends over for a party in a dirty house with a dirty pool, that was their problem. As embarrassed as I would be, I decided it was their party, not mine (Clarify and Accept). I decided not to yell or hound them but just wait and see what happened (Accept). Well, about three hours before the party, they realized what a mess everything was. I reminded them of our agreement and told them it would be teaching them a bad lesson if I bailed them out (Clarify). My oldest son called a friend who came over and helped clean the pool while the boys straightened up the house and picked up the yard. It wasn't perfect, but they did it themselves and I didn't have to nag or yell at them."

Hungry for an Argument

"I realized that my husband and I tend to get into arguments right after we get home from work. One or the other of us often has to work late and each of us expects the other to have some food ready when we get home (Clarify). We are both tired after a long day, and neither of us feels like doing much when we first get home. After learning about low blood sugar, I realized this might be a big part of our problem. I bought some snacks that we could eat as soon as we got home (Balance). Now we have a little routine which we both enjoy. The first one home gets out the snack and two glasses of wine. Then, when the other one gets home, we sit down and talk about our day and figure out what we want to do for dinner (Balance and Clarify). We eat a little later but a lot more peacefully."

Preventing an Argument

"My husband and I were waiting in line at the movies with some friends. My husband made a remark about me that really made me mad. Normally I would let this build up all night long and we would have a knock-down, drag-out when we got home. When we got into the theater, I started doing the Natural Rhythmic Breathing and pressed my feet into the floor (Balance). My husband offered to go get popcorn and drinks. I could see that he was feeling bad about what he said. After thinking about it, I realized that he had been trying to be funny but I didn't appreciate his doing it at my expense (Accept and Clarify). I was actually able to enjoy the movie, and we had a good time going dancing afterwards. When we got home, I told my husband I felt hurt by what he said (Clarify). He apologized and promised not to do it again."

Chapter Nineteen

Stress is a Choice

Stress Is Never Good for Us

It is well established that going through adversity can build character and endurance. That's not true about stress. In fact, I'm hard-pressed to think about anything good that can come out of stress and tension (except possibly an opportunity to recognize its negative effects). Adversity challenges our strength, creativity, and cooperative spirit. Stress and tension diminish our strength, block our creativity, and make us more self-centered. Adversity draws our focus. Stress scatters our focus. Anything that we do well under stress could be done better without stress.

If this is so, then why is stress so prevalent in these times? Young children are rushed and pressured to fulfill schedules overflowing with lessons, classes, and sports on top of school and never-ending mounds of homework. Senior citizens can get so busy that they say they don't have time to relax. Everyone in between seems to have more to do, and less time to do it in. From cradle to grave, we are pushed and driven to do more and more.

People under constant stress are less satisfied with their lives, have a diminished capacity for pleasure, have more trouble with relationships, poorer health, and are much more likely to be anxious or depressed than those who are able to keep stress at bay. Why do we do this?

I believe that is a very important question that we all need to think about. We tend to see stress as inevitable in this culture. One of the most common topics of everyday conversation is how busy and overworked we are. It has become an expectation that we will always have more to do than we have time to do it.

A Bad Trade Off

I cannot think of a situation where it's worth it to endure long-term stress for a greater good. It may be helpful to exceed our limits in a short-term emergency, but the costs of our diminished receptivity and awareness, as well as the mistakes we are likely to make, can never justify a stressful lifestyle. I worked with a woman who had been hospitalized after a severe panic attack at work. She had been in the same job with escalating stress for fifteen years. She worked for a small company, and forms authorizing everything that came into or went out of the organization had to cross her desk. She had been working ten-to-fourteen-hour days six or seven days per week when, finally, her body said "enough" and she was taken to the hospital in an ambulance.

She learned how to get into balance using the techniques described in this book. The week after she returned to work, she told me she had discovered a new way to organize her office that saved her more than two hours per day. She had been doing the same work for more than fifteen years and had never noticed this before. She said she had been so busy doing her job that she never thought about how she did it. Then, one of the first days back, she took a mid-afternoon break (which she never did before), and it came to her.

I believe that stress is a major factor in many divorces. Increasing tension restricts our sensitivity to, and awareness of, our partner, and spills over into everyday tasks and decision-making. As pressure and strain escalate, the person closest to us becomes the one most likely to bump into our emotional "sunburn." Sharing turns into confrontation. Discussion becomes argument. We see our spouse as the source of our stress and unhappiness when, in fact, those problems are around us and within us.

It is impossible to estimate the total cost of stress in our lives. We cannot begin to count the missed opportunities, lost relationships, or wasted potential that have resulted from being too stressed-out for too long. Stress not only diminishes our lives; it can shorten them as well. With stress, we get less for more.

Stress Is Not Inevitable

Stress is a choice. Unfortunately, it is the default choice in this culture. If we go with the flow and allow ourselves to be enticed by everyone who is trying to sell us something, we will either live a stressful life, feel like a failure, or both. However, we can choose not to be so stressed. It is not an easy choice. It requires us to go against the grain and swim upstream in a culture that doesn't support the concept of "good enough." Choosing to resist stress involves making balance a priority, letting go of the concept of "should," following through on what is most important, and accepting that we can't do or have everything we want without cost.

Living with less stress involves hard choices and a long-term commitment. The temptations for "more" in this culture are endless. It is up to each one of us to set limits on our lives. There will always be more we "could" do or have. We can choose to place our limits so we live with more stress or with less stress. By choosing less stress, we will have more quality in our lives, work, and relationships.

Stress-Free is As Easy as ABC

Becoming stress-free is not a distant fantasy. It is not even that complicated or difficult, but it does require consistent effort. The key is to start by stopping the build-up of tension in our body. That's because tension in our body pulls our mind toward negative thinking and blocks or intensifies emotion. Trying to control thinking or regulate emotion when physical tension is building is like trying to swim upstream in a strong current. I remember trying to swim against the flow in a fast moving river while canoeing up north. I had to work as hard as I could just to stay in the same place.

Practicing Natural Rhythmic Breathing (described in Chapter 11) six times per day for three to five minutes over two to six weeks takes our body out of fight or flight mode, restores balance to our autonomic nervous system, and clears stress hormones from our bloodstream. This allows us to respond rather than react to conflicts and challenges. Practicing grounding (Chapter 12) two to three times daily for the same period of time begins to break up patterns of tension and help us become aware of when tension first starts to build. Tension uses up energy and pulls our mind to dwell on the past and future. Resolving patterns of tension brings us back to the moment and frees this energy for more productive and enjoyable pursuits. It also helps us be more relaxed and flexible.

When our body is in balance, it is much easier to learn to control thinking (Chapter 13) and deal with emotion in a healthy way (Chapter 14). We can easily repeat a Thought Refocusing phrase hundreds of times per day by setting up simple reminders to use it whenever our mind is free. Doing this for a week or two establishes a pathway in our brain that we can easily switch to when we recognize that worry or negativity is interfering with our effectiveness and peace of mind. Establishing a daily practice of meditating twenty minutes per day helps us learn to recognize when our thoughts are counterproductive or building tension and provides us with the ability to refocus them in a helpful direction. Regular meditation helps us see a larger picture and relevant details more clearly. It becomes easier to see choices that fit the needs of the situation and are consistent with our values and priorities.

My students are required to practice Natural Rhythmic Breathing, Grounding, Thought Re-Focusing and Meditation for ten consecutive days in the middle of the semester. They consistently report that, even though it took up to an hour out of their day, they accomplished more in less time, with greater ease, more energy, and fewer problems. Test taking and grades improve with less studying. What seemed like major conflicts turn into speed bumps. Spouses, children, co-workers, and friends comment on how much nicer these students seem to be. Increased efficiency and effectiveness more than make up for time spent restoring and maintaining balance. Students report easily fitting maintenance practice into their daily routine after completing the assignment.

Starting with Balance makes it much easier to learn to apply the other ABC principles (Chapters 16-18). Practicing Acceptance is like preventing knots forming in string. Worry, pressure, blame, judgment, resentment and "should" easily twist thoughts and perceptions into a snarled mess that draws other people's knots like velcro. Acceptance prevents that. Accepting other people allows us to understand how they see and feel about things. It undermines defensiveness, minimizes reactivity, and leads to mutual respect. We work together rather than against each other to solve problems and resolve conflicts. Acceptance also helps us to realize that resisting pain and loss only intensifies discomfort. I have seen hundreds of people learn to experience severe pain and loss without building tension or creating stress by applying the ABC's.

Trying to think clearly when our body is in crisis mode is like driving in a storm with a fogged-up windshield and twisted mirrors. Stopping the build-up of tension clears the sky and windows and adjusts the mirrors so we can see where we are, where we've been, and where we want to go. Clarifying helps us to understand what's happening and sort out what's relevant and important while seeing what can realistically be accomplished. We become more able to acknowledge what we don't know and realize that life is an ongoing learning process.

Incorporating the ABC's into our daily lives forms habits that allow us to be at ease while being fully and completely ourselves. We begin to recognize our gifts and potential and to understand how stress affects and limits those around us. Functioning at full capacity without hurry or tension becomes our default condition. We learn to quickly spot obstacles to effective living and make choices that bring a sense of ease to work and relationships.

Choose Your Snowball

Stress quickly snowballs. Increasing tension makes us more reactive, pulls our mind toward the negative, and blocks or intensifies emotion. All these things add more tension while diminishing our capacity to see clearly and solve problems. We become less aware of our decreasing effectiveness as stress and pressure increase. This contributes to more problems and conflicts as it builds more tension. The snowball gets bigger and bigger and rolls faster and faster until we crash into something (often someone else's snowball) or collapse into a heap when we run out of momentum.

Choosing to work on becoming stress-free creates a snowball effect in the other direction. Reducing stress and tension restores our ability to function effectively and makes it easier to accept loss, anticipate and solve problems, and spot opportunities. It allows us to get a clearer picture of what's happening and to understand the perspective of those involved. Since conflicts are much easier to resolve before tension starts to build, we deal with them quickly and effectively. This reduces our stress and the stress of those around us, which prevents further problems and conflict. The result is increasing confidence, trust, and cooperation, which deepens our capacity to function effectively, and makes it easier to support each other and work together.

The stress snowball is the default choice. Habit and a high stress culture pull us in the direction of escalating tension. But we have the option to take a step back and choose a stress-free life of health and effectiveness. We can choose to move in the direction of increasing peace, joy, and fulfillment. We can choose to slow down and lighten up.

For additional information and videos that demonstrate and explain concepts and techniques described in this book, please visit www.bobvanoosterhout.com

Teachers and Educators
If you are interested in using this book for a course you teach, curriculum ideas, handouts, videos and discussion questions are available at http://www.bobvanoosterhout. com or send an email to bobvanoost@gmail.com

Reading Groups
Discussion topics are available at at http://www. bobvanoosterhout.com

Attention artists, writers, actors, programmers, teachers, and musicians

If you believe that the information in this book can help people can improve their lives and our world, please consider using your talents to help spread the message. I am interested in developing and providing links to videos, animation, short fiction, children's stories, songs, poetry, activities, and games that convey this and related material a larger audience who may not have the interest or opportunity to read this text.

For more information please visit http://www.bobvanoosterhout.com or send an email to bobvanoost@gmail.com

The Author

Bob Van Oosterhout is a Masters level psychologist and college professor who has been applying the approaches described in the book to real life situations since the early 1970's. He has a Masters Degree from Michigan State University, completed four years of post-graduate clinical training through the Michigan Society for Bioenergetic Analysis and is a limited licensed Psychologist (LLP) and Licensed Masters Social Worker (LMSW) through the State of Michigan. Bob has provided training for schools, corporations, small businesses, hospitals, health care clinics, professional organizations, as well as government and non-profit agencies. He recently retired from counseling at a rural health clinic in Northern Michigan. Bob was asked to develop a course in stress management for the Health Careers Department at Lansing Community College in 1981 and has been teaching it since that time. He has taught online since 2001.